THE
GANDHI EXPERIMENT

Margaret Hepworth is a Peace Educator; the Founder/Director of The Gandhi Experiment, whose vision is world peace through education. Her drive and commitment for social justice has grown and flourished through her secondary teaching of almost thirty years, and has now culminated in her workshops for students and adults. Margaret has been Head of Campus (Vice-Principal) at Preshil School, Melbourne, Australia and holds a Master of Educational Studies. She is the creator of *Collaborative Debating* and published her first novel, *Clarity in Time*, in 2012 through Balboa Press.

A vibrant presenter, she is well versed in public speaking, having facilitated workshops in Australia, India, Pakistan, Indonesia and Fiji. Her interesting and varied background includes travelling widely and having lived and taught in Melbourne, Australia, the USA, and Nanjing, China. Margaret is an expert in teenage motivations and behaviour.

In 2016, Margaret received the Sir John Monash Award for Inspirational Women's Leadership.

Above all, her belief in what she is trying to achieve—to help others step forward to make a difference in this world—gives Margaret the drive, passion and commitment required to help achieve peace through education.

Margaret currently resides in Melbourne, Australia.

Praise for the Book

This is a much needed text to return the world to its roots—peace education. Perfect for family and school environments, these activities and ideas are pivoted towards building a future based on the roots of sustainable peace.

—Kirthi Jayakumar, Author/Peace Activist

THE
GANDHI EXPERIMENT

Teaching our teenagers how to become global citizens

MARGARET HEPWORTH

RUPA

Published by
Rupa Publications India Pvt. Ltd 2017
7/16, Ansari Road, Daryaganj
New Delhi 110002

Sales Centres:

Allahabad Bengaluru Chennai
Hyderabad Jaipur Kathmandu
Kolkata Mumbai

Copyright © Margaret Hepworth 2017

The views and opinions expressed in this book are the author's own and the facts are as reported by her which have been verified to the extent possible, and the publishers are not in any way liable for the same.

All rights reserved.
No part of this publication may be reproduced, transmitted, or stored in a retrieval system, in any form or by any means, electronic, mechanical, photocopying, recording or otherwise, without the prior permission of the publisher.

ISBN: 978-81-291-4770-7

First impression 2017

10 9 8 7 6 5 4 3 2 1

The moral right of the author has been asserted.

Printed at Thomson Press India Ltd., Faridabad

This book is sold subject to the condition that it shall not, by way of trade or otherwise, be lent, resold, hired out, or otherwise circulated, without the publisher's prior consent, in any form of binding or cover other than that in which it is published.

When the sword becomes words,
Blaring guns morph–
peace is sung!
Then, my friend, thy will be done.

For Gandhi

Contents

Preface — *xi*
Introduction — *xv*
How to Read/Use this Book — *xxi*

One:	The Dinner Party to Save the World	1
Two:	The Best Forgiveness Role-Play Ever	43
Three:	The Utopian Scale	59
Four:	Einstein's Theory of Why? Why? Why?	72
Five:	The Conundrum of Inner Listening	86
Six:	The 'Call It What It Is' Theory of Life	105
Seven:	Almost Impossible Thoughts	118

Conclusion — 135
The Songlines — 139
Endnotes — 141
References — 147
Acknowledgements — 149

Preface

Too many people are experimenting with war and violence.
We need more people experimenting with peace and non-violence.

MARGARET HEPWORTH, May 2014

THE GANDHI EXPERIMENT: WHAT IS IN THE NAME?

In January 2014, after attending a 'Making Democracy Real' conference in Panchgani, India, I had a singular goal—to get to the Sabarmati Ashram, in Ahmedabad, the site of Gandhiji's second ashram in India. Travelling by train from Mumbai to Ahmedabad, thoughts raced through my head. Whilst everyone else slept, I scribbled notes, an emboldened woman. New ideas were flowing thick and fast about choices we make in life, about education alternatives, and about me.

At Sabarmati, I felt fortunate to meditate in the very same place that Gandhi had prayed morning and night. The ideas sown in the train grew, flourished, strengthened. I was excited! A new idea floated in through my meditative state—'You don't need to start a new movement. The movement is already out there. You just need to encourage it to grow.'

It was also at Sabarmati that a young Dutch couple wandered in. They looked around, read thoughtfully and carefully, then turned to one of the ashram curators and asked, 'Who was this Gandhi? What does he mean "My experiments with truth"?'

They had never heard of him. To be honest, I was taken aback. They'd never heard of Gandhi? I made a commitment, then, that when I returned home I would run my own 'experiments'. Subsequently and over time, I began by inviting many groups of students to tell me about Gandhi. They could tell me a little—'He was a peace-builder.' 'He was a social activist.' 'We think it was to do with the British.' 'He wore glasses.'

When I asked those same students to tell me about Hitler, well, they could talk for hours. They knew intricate details, family background, quotes, war atrocities, symbolism. I began to ask myself, 'How is it we seem to know more about the bad stuff and less about the good stuff?'

I returned to India in May the same year (2014), to attend the 'Education Today, Society Tomorrow, Initiatives of Change' conference. Afterwards I stayed in Delhi and visited Gandhi Smriti. Meditating on the fresh, green lawn facing the dignified Gandhi memorial, the name of my new educational project—a project that I believed would add new life to an ebbing educational world—came to me: The Gandhi Experiment. Later I courageously added: world peace through education.

REFLECTIONS ON AN AEROPLANE, 2015

The man seated three seats up and across the aisle from me has just watched six hours of violence through the in-flight movies. It began with *American Sniper*, then moved to some others I didn't recognize, where pigtailed men flaunted their prowess to kill savagely. Six hours of violence on a plane.

My eyes kept being drawn to, what was to me, soundless madness. My mind, however, was drawn to these thoughts—here I was, sitting in a plane, returning from a series of remarkable peace-building workshops across India. There was considerable irony here. I looked around at my fellow passengers. A number of Aussies sat close by, to my right two Americans, a few aisles up and to my left, sat two turbaned Sikhs. Quite a number of Chinese, a few Muslim veiled women, an Indian couple with no obvious-to-me visible markers to determine their religious orientation, a few heavily bearded men, myself, a Sai Baba pendant dangling from my neck, and Singaporean flight attendants beaming those award-winning smiles. With all this 'difference' aboard this plane, why weren't we all at each other's throats? Like in the movies? Instead we sat quietly, respectfully. Does peace exist only in certain contexts?

It's really a simple statement of fact. If all these people are able to coexist in a tight space for seven-and-a-half hours together without bickering, snarling, challenging, pushing, shoving, slapping, punching—if it is possible for an eclectic bunch of travellers to coexist peacefully together, then it is *possible* for this to happen anywhere; yes, anywhere in this world.

Perhaps a healthy dose of non-violent, solution-focused activities stemming from Gandhian principles, would be a more productive approach than subjecting ourselves to hours of contrived and stylized violence. Perhaps then our earth and all its occupants may experience a far more peaceful journey.

Both violence and non-violence are conscious choices. Throughout this book we will return to this learning again and again. When the anger swells, as it will, when conflicts arise, as they will continue to do so, we can teach people to choose non-violence. This doesn't mean people won't continue to get angry or upset. What it does mean is they will protect themselves from themselves and keep others safe.

As I travel with my workshops, I have been asking teenagers this question: Give me ten ways to stop violence through non-violence. The resulting lists have been worthy of Nobel Peace Prizes! Very real, very practical solutions applicable to the schoolyard, the family home, the community and to war and terrorism. A fifteen-year-old boy in Melbourne told me, 'We need to ask our enemy, "What is your truth?"' That's about as 'Gandhi' as it gets!

Why are we working with teenagers? A long-term vision for world peace requires current prevailing attitudes to shift. We can achieve this through overt education. However, here is another reason. As adults, we have so much to learn from our teenagers when we allow them to use their voices.

The Gandhi Experiment teaches teenagers global citizenship, conflict resolution, anger management, forgiveness and how to enact their thoughts for a more positive future. Over-arching this learning, we teach, 'Change begins with me.' It may well teach you the same.

Introduction

Every teenager knows that the world needs to change.

THEORIES, CONCEPTS AND PRACTICES UNDERPINNING THIS BOOK

Teenagers can be the most altruistic people on the planet. Given the right opportunities they are engaged, active, and positive. Let's unlock this potential, whilst utilizing a number of educational theories and practices at school and at home.

I am no longer asking 'Is Gandhi still relevant today in education?' Having held The Gandhi Experiment workshops across Melbourne, Australia, India, Pakistan and Fiji, my experience tells me that the answer is a resounding 'Yes'.

The Gandhi Experiment is not about the man himself. It is about the essence of his message:

- Non-violence as a conscious choice;
- 'Satyagraha', truth or soul-force—understanding that when 'my' truth does not match 'your' truth we never use violence as an answer;
- Getting off our backsides to take action about injustices

and those things we know need to change. Where 'Hope in action' and 'Moving from apathy to action' become our maxims. Nelson Mandela told us, 'We all need to rise beyond our own expectations of ourselves'. This is what The Gandhi Experiment invites us to do;

- Change begins with me. The toughest realization is not, 'I can see where he or she needs to change', it is: 'I can see where I need to change';
- 'My life is my message', I will live my life through my values.

I have combined these 'Gandhi' messages with theories, concepts and practices I use in my own classrooms, outlined below. They underpin all the activities in this book. As a teacher with nearly thirty years under my belt, I use these concepts to engage, provide equity for all students and to make the learning 'stick', so it is applied well beyond the classroom. I have chosen seven to outline here. A growing resource-list can be found on my website[1], if you wish to read further in a particular area.

The More Teenagers Know and Understand Themselves, the Better Life Is For Them

The better life is for them, the better it is for everyone around them. This is one of my own maxims. Through overt learning, we help young people understand their own behaviour and reasons for doing things. One such theory, Howard Gardner's Multiple Intelligences, allows teachers to realize their students' potential through the different learning

---

[1] www.thegandhiexperiment.com

styles of those sitting right before us in our classrooms. But that knowledge shouldn't just sit with us as the teacher; our students should know this about themselves too. 'What is the way in which I learn best? How can I apply this to my studies?' Combine this with 'Strengths Education', and we are inculcating a love of learning.

Let's Employ Some Critical Thinking

Teach a meta-cognitive approach—to think about our thinking, to learn about our learning; to understand that we are constructs of our time, place and culture. Let's understand how texts position us to think and respond in a particular way. Let's get brave enough to even allow our teenagers to challenge us! Let's hold courageous conversations!

Not Everyone has to Achieve the Same Group Goal the Same Way

We don't all have to go to an old-age home to learn to be of service to others. The concept of 'Parallel Thinking' derived by Edward de Bono states that by laying ideas down in parallel, we can move towards the same goal, but 'I will do it my way, whilst you can do it your way.' We are teaching the group, and yet creating an individual's passioned response. When we help our teenagers understand their passion, their skills, their expertise, and combine this with value education, we are encouraging young people to step into their futures, accepting differing attitudes, with the ability to make wiser choices. If our common goal is 'to make the world a better place', there are many different pathways we can walk to achieve this.

Flood their Minds with Hope

Positive psychology has shed 'new light' on something teachers have always observed in working with teenagers. When faced with overwhelm, layers and layers of negativity—too much of the 'bad stuff' that is happening out there—young people are more inclined to throw up their hands, 'give in' and move to a point of despair and apathy. If, however, whilst still being made aware of community and global issues, teenagers are also taught about the 'good stuff'—the number of people finding solutions and taking action for positive change—these very same young people move to a point of action and positive engagement themselves. Hope stimulates action; action spurs hope. This concept is explored in Chapter Three, 'The Utopian Scale'.

People Need to Feel Something Before They Will Do Anything About a Situation

The use of carefully-framed provocations, designed to stimulate a response, not only create healthy dialogue, they lead to action. This style of teaching ensures the learning will be embedded and will stay with our teenagers for years to come.

We Need to Demonstrate a Different Way of Thinking

Here we are employing Einstein's mantra: 'We cannot solve our problems with the same thinking that we used to create them.' For example, instead of, 'We own the planet' (a paradigm often embedded in the psyche of large corporations), we need to shift to 'We are custodians of the planet.' In fact the latter concept has existed for millennia within our tribal nations across the planet. Think about the shift in a worldly perspective when we move from 'I win, you lose,' to 'When I win, you win too.'

Belonging

Child psychologists tell us that one of the largest influences on young people is the need to 'belong'. As teachers and parents, it is incumbent on us to help every child feel they belong to a positive, inclusive group.

Utilizing the Power of Creative Energy in a Classroom

To enjoy teaching teenagers, means to be *in joy* with these young people; working with their energetic flow.

Gandhi and his compatriots conceived of a 'basic education for all,' naming it 'Nai Talim'. This is sometimes interpreted as 'New education' or 'Education for life.' The philosophy of Nai Talim, whilst set in the context of a British-indentured India, put forth that 'education was not a narrow means of making careers and achieving social status, but also the seeking of a larger role for self and society' (www.gandhifoundation.net).

Whilst I have re-contextualized for a different era, much of what was being sought through Nai Talim is espoused in the pages of this book. Martin Luther King Jr possibly best summed up Gandhi's views: 'Intelligence plus character; that is the goal of true education.' This is the much needed 'Value Education' or 'Peace Education'.

Out beyond the stifled classroom, the jaded learning,
there is a field,
I will meet you there.

RUMI MEETS HEPWORTH

How to Read/Use this Book

To successfully use these activities at home or in the classroom, we are relying on your professionalism, teaching and parenting skills to read through each chapter first; be very familiar with the material.

Make decisions about how you would use each activity in your particular context, environment, student groups, family situation; you need to 'adjust' the teaching according to your cohort of teenagers. You can add video clips, new readings and your own knowledge and expertise as a teacher or parent.

You do not need to move through the book in the order of chapters. They are distinct, 'stand alone' activities, yet the concepts are intertwined.

However, three chapters in this book —should be completed in one session, taking students from a starting point to a light-bulb moment, or a moment of deep personal realization—a transformation. These are best done in one 'sitting'. They may however, require longer than a typical one class period.

These chapters are:

'The Best Forgiveness Role-Play Ever'
'The Utopian Scale'
'Almost Impossible Thoughts'

Once 'completed', you can then create highly effective ongoing individualized projects in your classroom or at home.

Three other chapters—contain a number of activities based on one overarching concept being taught in that chapter. These activities can therefore be spaced over time.

You will see that with some of these, the same activity can be used over and over again. It is through practice that we grow as experts in any area. In practising the techniques used here, our teenagers will come to know and understand themselves in a way that will allow them to make powerful and positive choices.

'Einstein's Theory of Why? Why? Why?'
'The Conundrum of Inner Listening'
'The "Call It What It Is" Theory of Life'

As for the first chapter, The Dinner Party to Save the World, I have 'played' this in various ways: over a two-hour period, over an entire day, and also segmented over a number of sequential classroom lessons. You can decide how best to structure the 'Dinner Party' to meet the constraints of time.

Any and all of these activities can continue to be raised in your classrooms. Above all, utilize the buoyant humour and energy of teenagers to make these activities vital, life learning, transformative experiences.

One

The Dinner Party to Save the World

GANDHI was a thinker, a talker and a doer. Thoughts elicited through prayer, meditation, quiet time and discussion came to life with a force and vitality that ensured response and directed action. In a very real sense, Gandhi held many 'Dinner parties to save the world.' No, not the socialite variety! Constantly meeting with colleagues, politicians, friends and strangers, he invested time into public and private conversations. Whilst his primary focus was on India, his message was, and still is, for the world.

This chapter invites you into an imagined dinner party where thirteen people have gathered. Their purpose—to discuss how best to save the world. Whether a 'guest' at the Dinner Party or the host, you are not being told what to think; you are being invited *to think*! No longer a passive listener, you are asked to become a critical thinker. As you listen to the conversations at this pretend dinner party, you will be inspired to have your own conversations, at your own 'party', with students, peers, friends, colleagues or family. The outcome could be priceless.

I imagine Gandhiji's conversations were real and

courageous. They weren't a cursory pat on the back, sharing a joke or two, and then sidling back to a place of inaction. Even those whose opinions sat on the other side of the table, such as Lord Reading, then British Viceroy of India, spoke of Gandhi as being direct—'There is no hesitation about him and there is a ring of sincerity in all that he utters.'

In British Prime Minister Churchill's demonization of Gandhi as the 'seditious fakir', we sense his frustration in coming face to face with someone who staunchly would not bow under pressure—even that of the 'mighty British Empire'.

I want you to carefully consider the implications of the following anecdote about a well-known repartee, though it is not well-documented as to when it actually occurred. Gandhi alighted in London to be met by an enthusiastic reporter, delighted to have this opportunity to showcase both his talent as a journalist and his pride in his British heritage. Addressing this fragile man dressed in swaddling clothes, the journalist asked, 'So Mr Gandhi, what do you think of Western Civilization?'

Gandhi replied, 'I think it would be a good idea.'

Gandhi's response, and the 'Dinner Party,' are designed to make us think, to question, to see our own lives in a new light—the good, the bad, the ugly and the indifferent. To ask—What is my role in all that is going on around me? Do I need to step away from it, hide from it, or step up to it? Do I need to face up to my own responsibility? Do I need to better understand my connection to all things in this world?

'The Dinner Party to Save the World' is a call to explore much-needed conversations for today, to invest our time for our future, but also a call to commitment and action.

Nelson Mandela, himself a proponent of Gandhi's teaching and methodology, told us, 'We all need to step up beyond our own expectations of ourselves.' The Dinner Party to Save the World invites you to step up.

WHAT INFLUENCE DID GANDHI WIELD THAT MILLIONS HEEDED HIS CALL?

If you seek to make a positive difference, then learn how to work through body, mind and spirit, just as Gandhi did. Through the use of the mind, Gandhi articulated arguments through the legal system, held countless conversations with politicians, and published articles in his own publications, attempting to sway others and spread his ideas.

Through the body we observe his ability to both sit still—which allowed him to listen to his voice of inner guidance (which we explore in Chapter Five)—and yet be active beyond imagination. His campaigns of non-cooperation saw millions of people flooding the jail system, many staying strong, choosing non-violence over a raised fist or weapon.

And through spirit he derived some of the most formidable challenges to the British. One example of this is the symbolic Salt March of 1930 he led in blatant disregard of British law that disallowed Indians to make their own salt.

Imagine being sixty-year old Gandhi, walking those 390 km. The idea came to him in his quiet time, his 'stilled silence'. His ability to find and be guided by his inner voice, was perhaps his greatest and yet most unheralded achievement. This is one of the keys to inner peace. And inner peace is the key to peace within the community. For Gandhi, body, mind and spirit were intertwined[1]: 'India gives me the spiritual governance I need'; 'Submission to a state wholly or largely unjust is an immoral barter for liberty. Thus considered, civil resistance is a most powerful expression of a soul's anguish.'

Gandhi Appealed to 'The Multiple Intelligences'

Interestingly Gandhi was appealing, whether he knew it or not, to what educationist Howard Gardner termed the 'multiple intelligences', in other words, to our preferred learning styles. Gandhi had created a movement relatable to the academic, the philosopher, the doer, and the spiritualist; the greatest power of which lay in his insistence that character underpinned every thought and action.

Thus his appeal touched the audio, the visual and the kinaesthetic learners; the academics, the physically intelligent, the 'nature-smart', the intra-personal and the inter-personal; and to what my son, James Tyler terms, the Consciousness Intelligent—those who understand and resonate with the deeper meaning of being 'awake'.

Gandhi was indeed a rebel with a cause. As a rebel seeks not to cooperate with the system, his was a non-cooperation with injustice. To those engaged in the movement to de-colonize India, it must have felt that the basic tenets of all religions— love, peace, kindness and non-violence were rhetoric no longer. They were actually being practiced!

As you play out your Dinner Party to Save the World,

---

[1]Excerpts taken from, Fischer L., (1983), Ed., *The Essential Gandhi: An Anthology of His Writings on His Life, Work, and Ideas*, pp. 143–144, Vintage Spiritual Classics, Random House: New York.

keep these questions in mind:

- How can we use the multiple intelligences to engage our learners in the Dinner Party?
- How do we explore different pathways for different people, ostensibly leading to the same goal—to make this world a better place for all?
- How do we, in this different day and age, actively choose to not cooperate with injustice?
- We will need to think deeply and laterally, to open our eyes to our own connection with injustice—seen and unseen—to become honest about the role we play.

So let's hold our own 'Dinner Party', and whilst we do, let's remember to uphold two more of Gandhi's qualities—humour and tenacity. For, even a simple dinner together can lead to conflict, argument and vehement differences of opinion. Remember tenacity—the ability to stay with it, to see it through even when the going gets tough. Oh, and remember always—non-violence!

LESSON PLAN

The Dinner Party to Save the World begins with an invitation. Send it out to all those 'invited'.

Dear _____,

If somebody invited you to help save the world, would you do it? Would you think, 'Seriously? I can't do that. Isn't that a job best left for the big guys: the scientists, the researchers, the politicians, the people who know how to do that stuff? Besides, I'm a bit busy on that night.'

If somebody invited you to save a whale, would you do it? Phone call. It's your good friend, Samina 'A whale has washed up on the back-beach. Can you help come and save it? We need all hands on deck. Now!' Would you say, 'I'm sorry Samina. I don't know how to save a whale'? No, of course you would go.

The question is why would you go? Weren't you too busy on that night? What made you call off that coffee with Lisa, whom you hadn't caught up with, in months, and race off to rescue some whale that had never made your acquaintance? Why? Why would you go?

Would you go to save that animal because you felt some sense of humanitarian duty? Would you go for the adventure and the feeling that now, finally, you were really helping? Would you go, understanding that your individual effort would probably mean nothing standing on its own? But that a combined effort, if you and Samina and the others who had answered the call as you did, could together keep pouring water on this massive creature, that together you would dig a trench to provide life-giving water running along its side, that together you would continue your work, for hours if need be, until the high tide came in, lifting the animal and thereby allowing it to help itself?

You could do that. But are you a scientist? Are you a researcher? Do you need a degree to help save a whale? Do you need a degree to help save the world? No, all you need is permission from yourself.

You are cordially invited to attend a Dinner of Discourse/Debate/Discussion.

> *Don't think too much about the dinner, more about the debate. Food is not the main course; rather thoughts will be dissected, chewed up, swallowed and hopefully spat out at some other end.*
>
> *When you eat the food, enjoy it for its delicious and nutritious properties, however, it does after all, diminish in size after each bite. Thought, on the other hand, can also be enjoyed and yet can flourish in abundance post ingestion.*

Tell your 'Dinner Guests' to—'bring your own drinks, brain, heart, soul and your sense of humour but leave the cynicism and unconstructive comments at the door with your shoes'.

Having a Dinner Party

In the Classroom

Use the following script as a springboard for your students to engage in their own discussions about each of the issues presented. This may, in turn, lead to further issues they feel are relevant. For example, I once ran The Dinner Party to Save the World over three consecutive lessons at the end of a unit of work on Food Security and students were able to discuss what they had learned.

Use the script to hold conversations, then ask each student to create a poster representing a particular cause they are interested in. Create research projects through group work on each of the various topics presented. An entire unit of work on 'Sustainability' can grow out of The Dinner Party—a unit of work that promotes action.

Allow your students to share healthy food as they discuss. This in itself is a 'lesson'. What is understood to be 'healthy food'? This could also open a conversation about respecting each other's cultural and religious food choices.

In the Family Home

Invite your children into the most needed discussion of the 21st century. How best can we save the world? What does it mean 'to save the world'? To add depth, make your guest list intergenerational—invite their grandparents, aunts, uncles, cousins, neighbours. You decide.

In a Restaurant or Community Hall

The Dinner Party to Save the World can be held within a two- to three-hour period, whilst actually sharing a delightful community dinner with a large group of people. Select a few topics from the Dinner Party script.

Commitment and Outcome

It is important to note that whichever scenarios you choose, the outcome should be the same—that each participant makes a personal commitment to their next steps towards making a positive difference. The premise we are working with: We wish to meet reality head on and yet the focus, or the shift, must be 'hope in action'.

We are creating and building a sense of altruism, a self-less concern for others and for the planet. Each child, each person has innate peace-building skills. Let's help them flourish.

The Structure

Having invited all the guests through the invitation, and once all are gathered, the Dinner Party begins with the Entrée, continues into the Main Course, and culminates with Dessert: Time to Make a Commitment

Entrée

Welcome all the 'guests' and explain the structure of the evening. Encourage people to get to know each other by finding a partner and sharing a story. Tell them to share with each other on, 'What do you expect this evening /these "lessons" will be all about?'

Main Course

There are four main topics (in script form) outlined below for the 'main course'. Depending on your time availability, number and age of participants, you can select how many and which topics you will take on. Read the script out loud to all participants, remembering these are guests at an imagined dinner party. Their ages range from 12–42. You get to hear their conversations, then create your own. At the end of each section of script, stop to ask the question/provocations/activities. Essentially, these are starting points from which to springboard the conversations.

Do not be bound by the questions and instructions given here, you may tailor the questions after each topic to be as relevant to your particular audience as possible. We are opening up ideas and possibilities. Human creativity is as boundless as the universe—utilize it now.

The teacher/host should pre-read the script and facilitate the discussion. The teacher/host can sometimes choose to play the devil's advocate, but should state this as a position when doing so. The scenarios may also reference a short film-clip to watch, a visual to discuss, or other material to broaden the conversations. And finally, you will need to judge the time available to examine each topic.

Script 1: Waste

Read the script out loud.

> 'So,' I stated, 'we've come here to save the world. How are we going to do it?'
>
> The group had moved through dips and banter to the dining room, where we were now all seated around the walnut table, ready to tuck into our famous home-made pumpkin soup. I had brought the conversation to a screeching halt.
>
> Our guests looked around at each other, seemingly summing each person up, aware of their own knowledge base and authority, and yet suddenly sensing their own limitations.
>
> 'Er, that's a mighty big task, Rosie,' ventured Saurav.
>
> 'Yeah, I know. But if we don't ask where are we ever going to get? We can sit back and be complacent. We can criticize everything going on around us or we can choose to become truly constructive.'
>
> 'Right,' said Jacques enthusiastically, 'let's get started. I vote we break it down into manageable chunks. Not pureed, like the soup,' he said, dipping his soup spoon into

his bowl. 'Bite sized chunks is what we are looking for.'

'More like the carrots,' said Saurav, waving a carrot stick vigorously.

'Precisely.'

'I'm going to toss in one small idea and see where we head from there,' Jacques employed a more serious air. 'Personally, I'm tired of big corporations thinking it is a great idea to promote themselves by handing out plastic junk at events. This is something I get really angry about. This stuff is...well...it's rubbish! It takes energy to create it. Kids bring it home, it clutters up our houses. Eventually you throw it out. It goes straight to the landfill! The last time I took my nephews to a cricket match every kid got handed a large plastic hand. It was incredibly annoying because the little boy in front of me kept waving this "hand", which was just plastic rubbish, in my face! At the end of the game my nephews were out scavenging autographs and Bang! We thought someone was letting off firecrackers. It turns out that some of the kids had figured out that if you jump on these inflated plastic hands, they burst. It started a chain reaction. Bang, bang, bang! The next thing you know these "hands" were being popped all over the place. I looked around—hundreds and hundreds, perhaps thousands of exploded plastic all over the cricket ground. More tons of plastic straight to the tip. All this rubbish, all this waste; and what good does it do the world?'

'Good example,' I replied. 'I reckon, Gandhi would say use your anger to compel you to do something positive. Don't harbour your anger; take action. So, what are you going to do about the plastic hands and other tinkery stuff?'

'I'm not sure what I can do,' Jacques began. 'I guess I could begin by refusing to accept it when they hand it out? I could write a letter to the newspaper, stating my beliefs; trying to convince others not to accept it?' He looked to me as though to see if that was the 'correct' response.

'Cool and maybe another letter to the companies creating the stuff. Asking them to find another way to advertise. I realize they think they are making people happy but in reality they're only adding to the problem.'

Questions

Ask your students/guests:

- Have you ever had this type of experience—where plastic items or other materials are handed out like this, essentially for advertising a particular brand?
- What do you think about this?
- Do you see it as a problem like Jacques does?
- Have you ever thought about this before?
- What could be done about this?

Watch a video clip such as The Great Pacific Garbage Patch. https://www.youtube.com/watch?v=1qT-rOXB6NI

There are many clips you could use here. This one is particularly good in that it really makes people feel something, beyond just knowing the facts. Remember, it is when people feel something that they will shift to a point of action.

Now ask:

- What are some of the facts presented in the video clip?
- What does this make you think?
- How does it make you feel?
- What can we do about this?
- What is 'excessive materialism'? (You could show pictures here of materialism)
- If you take an honest look around your own house, do you think you are caught up in 'excessive materialism'?

On your paper, draw a line scale of 1–10. With 1 being minimum and 10 being maximum. Place an x where you think you sit on the 'materialism scale'? Remember, we are not looking to blame or create guilt, but we are looking for responsibility and a growing awareness.

Script 2: Food Sources/Our Carbon Footprint

Read the script out loud.

> The group had been discussing whaling—both Japanese whalers and those in Denmark—the Grind. Adam began very quietly. Never wanting to offend, but in the midst of the evening's discussion, he had found a new voice. 'How can you judge whalers when you put meat on your fork?'
>
> Jorge asked sarcastically, 'How can you even compare the two? Whales are sentient beings.'
>
> 'What—and cows and sheep are joyfully queuing up for the slaughter? Look, obviously I totally agree with you about the whales; it is very wrong, completely unnecessary and very likely having untold detrimental

effects on the oceans. I know one piece of advice the world hasn't listened to,' Adam continued bravely. 'Or some of us have. Well, many of you may not know that Einstein, back in the 1950s decided that we should all be vegetarians.'

'Einstein? Vegetarian? Are you sure?' queried Jorge.

'Give me a minute...Let me find it.' Adam pulled out his Smartphone and began plugging in letters. 'Ah, here 'tis. Einstein on vegetarianism. And I quote, "Nothing will benefit human health and increase the chances of survival of life on this Earth as much as the evolution to a vegetarian diet."'

'Really? Give me that.' Jorge read it for himself. 'So, was Einstein a vegetarian?' he asked, handing Adam back his phone.

'I believe he became one in the last few years of his life.'

'Probably what killed him!'

'Jorge!' This from Smita.

Adam pressed on. 'Listen to this.' He flicked down through the Googled quotes. 'Einstein also said, "Our task must be to free ourselves...by widening our circle of compassion to embrace all living creatures and the whole of nature and its beauty."'

'Doesn't that mean I should be compassionate towards this carrot?' Saurav asked, waving yet another orange morsel in his hand.

'I've got one!' I yelled, waving my iPad. 'A Gandhism: "The greatness of a nation and its moral progress can be judged by the way its animals are treated". Hey Sid, that's the quote you used with your final Art assignment last year.'

Sid answered sheepishly, 'Yes Rosie.'

'You should be proud of that artwork Sid.' I turned to the group. 'His photographic study was taken after the BP oil spill. It was called "BP look what you've done to me." He covered himself in "oil" to see or understand how it felt.'

Sid said, 'I was trying to show that if it affected the birds and animals it was also affecting us. And that we won't stop doing stupid and careless things until we really suffer the consequences ourselves.'

'Excellent concept, Sid,' said Akira, proud of the young boy whom she had known all his life, now emerging a young man.

'Yeah Siddy.' Adam reached forward and ruffled his younger brother's hair.

'Can I show everyone the photos?' I asked brightly.

'Ros-ie! No.'

'Maybe later,' I winked around the room.

'Oh my God!' Smita, who had been reading over my shoulder, had taken the iPad from my hands. She read out loud, '"For as long as men massacre animals, they will kill each other. Indeed, he who sows the seed of murder and pain cannot reap joy and love." Who do you think said that?' She looked at each of our faces, knowing she held the upper hand.

'Mandela?'

'No, much, much earlier.'

'Umm—Jesus the Vegan?'

'Pythagoras!' yelped Smita. 'And that was two-and-a-half thousand years ago! Seriously, how far haven't we come since then?'

'Pythagoras? The mathematician who made us do all those equations in Maths classes!' exclaimed Sid. 'What's he doing jabbering about animals. I thought he only cared about triangles!'

'That is Pythagoras the mathematician. One and the same, who also happened to be the founder of his own religion,' stated HJ dryly. 'Pythagoreanism. He believed, amongst other things, in reincarnation.'

Realizing that the conversation was going off track, Adam threw down a challenge. 'You meat eaters, you use up too much land. You allow too much farting of methane and ammonia—and nitrous oxide from cow poo for that matter! You hide the slaughter to shield yourselves from the blood, the reality of the killing. You allow the degeneration of land through churning hooves across the natural environment. You kill off native species by clearing land for your livestock. For God's sake, they're clearing the Brazilian rainforest—the lungs of the earth—for you meat eaters!'

Everyone sat there bemused and bewildered. Nobody had ever heard the eternally jovial and placid Adam speak like this. Gandhi was seeping through his veins. 'I wonder what would happen,' he continued firmly, 'if even half the developed world went vegetarian. Or even a third. Ha! It would have to make a difference. We would be saving you meat-eating lot and you wouldn't even know it!'

Jacques was busily offering more soup to those who chose. 'Vegetarian,' he grinned indicating the pot.

Questions

Provocation: 'Move to show what you think.'

- Create a semicircle in the room. With the extreme left being vegan, and the extreme right being meat-eaters, place yourself at a point along the semicircle where your beliefs currently sit. Once people have moved and arranged themselves in the semicircle, ask the following question: 'Should we all become vegetarian?'
- Allow people to cast any and all opinions on this. It is surprising how vehement people can become about this topic. Once the discussion has finished, request that people 'Move to show what you think,' again, with the extreme left being vegan and the extreme right being meat-eaters. 'Has anyone been swayed by this discussion? Would you now change your place on the semicircle continuum? If so why? What has influenced you?'
- Ask, what does the phrase 'our carbon footprint' mean? You can explore this concept with some quick internet research. 'Why should we concern ourselves with our own carbon footprint?'
- Discuss the perceived need of many scientists and researchers that humans will have to change their eating habits for sustainability of the planet.

Examples to explore:

- Did you know that over two billion people eat insects every day as part of their normal diet?' Select clips from 'Can eating insects save the world. https://www.youtube.com/watch?v=Acxbx-DUkL4
- What difference would it make to our carbon footprint if we were all eating insects? How do you feel about that? How is eating insects any different to eating prawns?
- Explore the search for new food sources—super foods. Look at examples of rooftop gardens/community gardens.
- Browse the internet for the quotes mentioned in this passage. Find other quotes about vegetarianism. Discuss.
- Discuss these as philosophical arguments: 'For as long as men massacre animals, they will kill each other. Indeed, he who sows the seed of murder and pain cannot reap joy and love' (Pythagoras); and 'The greatness of a nation and its moral progress can be judged by the way its animals are treated' (Gandhi).

Re-read aloud Adam's final rant.

> You meat eaters, you use up too much land. You allow too much farting of methane and ammonia—and nitrous oxide from cow poo for that matter! You covert yourselves from the slaughter to shield you from the blood, the reality of the killing. You allow the degeneration of land through churning hooves across

the natural environment. You kill off native species by clearing land for your livestock. For God's sake, they're clearing the Brazilian rainforest—the lungs of the earth—for you meat eaters!

What is he talking about? If you are using this in a classroom, you may like to research the causes behind the cutting down of the Brazilian Rainforest—the number one cause being cattle farming (for each pound of beef produced, 200 square feet of rainforest is destroyed).

Play 'Move to show what you think' again. See if anyone's position has changed post-research.

Show these visuals:

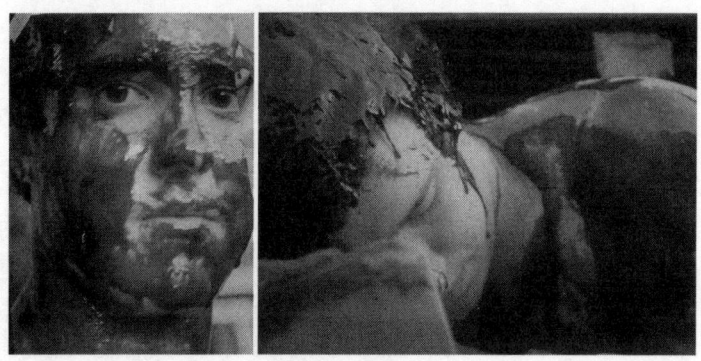

'BP Look what you've done to me.'
Art credit: James Tyler / Photo credit: Darcy Tyler

Ask: 'BP Look what you've done to me. What does Sid mean by saying, "We won't stop doing stupid and careless things until we really suffer the consequences ourselves"?'

Script 3: Overpopulation

Read the script out loud.

> 'I'm going to be brave and cast my opinion into the pot, so to speak,' said the quiet Inas. 'It is my belief that one of the biggest dilemmas facing us is our ever-expanding population. I believe that as part of our carbon footprint we should be moving towards zero population growth. You have one child to replace you on this earth. In other words, a couple has two children. And that's it. No more! These are the dilemmas we face. We want democracy, but democracy is only going to work if we make choices that benefit us as a collective; when we stop worrying about "me" and "mine" and start thinking about the "us". Look, I'm not saying that we don't already do this to some extent. But we don't do it consistently or often enough. We need a stronger altruistic voice in this community. More than what the politicians are offering us.'
>
> Jorge was stunned. 'You cannot possibly be telling us how many children we should be having?' He looked furtively around the table, trying to leverage support. 'That's a human rights issue! China imposed a One-Child Policy on its people years ago. It's not democratic. We have rights here, Inas. And besides, "we" are not the problem. It's those other countries that need better education on overpopulation!' He spoke challengingly, almost taunting the younger Inas, thrusting his large frame across the table.
>
> 'It's not all about you!' said HJ, stepping in to lend Inas support. 'No, I take it back. It *is* all about you—and

how you think and behave and act! It's about you and it's also about everyone else! It's not just about us and our corner of the world. It's about—well, it's about the world, the whole world.'

The room had fallen silent as HJ's words sank in. I felt his words, strong and empowering. And now HJ's anger was catching on. We have a right to be angry about this stuff, I thought. What was it that Gandhi had said? Satyagraha; Truth Force. A truth that you would march for, a truth that needed placards and stomping demands. Lots of yelling! A truth that you would die for. Okay, so I wasn't so sure about that part!

'People in "greenhouses" should throw stones!' I declared. 'Well,' I paused, 'metaphorical ones anyway.' I stopped. Spying at a few hot faces I said, 'Look what's happening. And we've only made it through soup!'

Questions

Provocation/activity: You may like to use the provocation on the two-child policy outlined below to engage real emotion about this controversial topic.

- The original quote is 'People who live in glasshouses shouldn't throw stones.' What does that mean? What does Rosie mean when she says, 'People in "greenhouses" should throw stones? Well, metaphorical ones anyway.'

    Example of a Provocation:

- Ask your class: 'Did anyone hear on the news this

morning that the government has announced that India (or insert your country here) is introducing a two-child policy in two years' time?'
- Invite opinions: 'What do you think of the idea that our government would be instituting a policy that stipulates how many children you can have i.e. two?' (Please note: You haven't actually told a lie and said this is happening. You have simply asked 'Did anyone hear this in the news this morning?')
- 'How might this impact you personally?'
- 'How might it impact our country?'
- 'Which is the only country in the world that has ever enforced a one-child policy (the answer, of course, is China)? Why would China have done this? What effect has it had on their country?'
- Allow your students to explore their immediate reactions to the concept of a two-child policy in their country: thoughts, feelings, reactions. Then, reveal to them, the reality. 'Did anyone hear on the news this morning that the government has announced that India (or your country) will be introducing a two-child policy in two years' time? Well, no, of course you didn't because it isn't real or true. Why might I have framed the debate in this way? (Meta-cognition.) We are, however, going to hold a debate about this very topic.'
- 'The proposition for our debate is: *India (or your country) should introduce a two-child policy.*'

  Teacher's note: To engage in healthy, non-adversarial debate that aims to find a solution to the problem, see

Collaborative Debating at www.thegandhiexperiment.com. The debate will be organized as two teams of three, alternating speakers from each team. The Affirmative team speaks in support of the proposition; the Cooperative team speaks against the proposition.

- 'What is zero population growth? What do you think/feel about this?' Allow time for considered discussion; encourage discussion on the pros and cons of a two-child policy and 'rights' as opposed to 'responsibilities' of human beings.
- Discuss Negative Population Growth. 'Some people see this as a human rights abuse—to be told that you can legally only have one child. Other people view the effects of over-population (poverty, lack of education for all, pollution, etc.), as a human rights abuse. What do you think?'
- 'There are now over seven billion people on this planet. Is rampant population growth sustainable? What is your role in all of this?'
- 'Should we be waiting for our governments to create laws to make us respond to what is needed?'
  Notice what happens when people *feel* something instead of being emotionally distant from the concept they are discussing. Notice the passion and intensity of the discussion when it becomes 'real' to them/pertinent to their lives. Ask them why they don't feel this when it is a reality in other people's lives?
- Discuss HJ's rage: 'It is all about you and your attitudes.' What does he mean?

Script 4: Attitudes

Read the script out loud.

> On returning to the dinner table, carrying in le pièce de résistance—the Moroccan curry—things appeared to have settled a little. The group had fallen to chatting amongst themselves, though Inas was still casting wary glances in Jorge's direction. Jacques helped serve the delectable curry and rice into clean bowls. Noses around the room heralded the delicious flavours that were soon to descend upon taste buds and stomachs.
>
> 'I want to ask you all a fairly esoteric question I have been pondering for some time now.' I drew the group back together as HJ and I resumed our seats. 'I've been seriously contemplating the ignominy of Human arrogance.'
>
> 'Big word, Rosie,'
>
> 'Big thoughts, Saurav!' I paused and continued. 'I mean, for example, how can we possibly say we are more important than ants? If you remove all the ants from a rainforest, the whole forest is corrupted, and will possibly die! How can we be more important than that? Or maybe we, as humans, are more important than one ant but less important than an entire forest of ants? Or are we the ants of the world? If you removed all humans from this earth, would the whole earth die? Or flourish? Or simply change form? My answer is I don't know,' I sighed.
>
> Twelve-year old Hisashi spoke clearly, 'But if you did know, what would the answer be?'
>
> With that query, Hisashi had suddenly and

unwittingly displaced my fear and unleashed my resolve. 'I believe that if we can all begin to think differently, if we really can gain a better sense of a collective human consciousness, then the world will change. I know you're thinking, well done! Of course it will because if we all manage to do this, then logically it follows that we will all be supporting green projects: buying the solar panels, putting money behind environmental research, etc. That's the physical upshot of the exercise. But I believe, there's more to it than that. There has to be a more spiritual element to it.' I could see Jorge rolling his eyes. Agh, here she goes again. Off on her Dalai-lama-isms.

'I'm not saying we need to become religious. There's a massive difference between following religious dogma and being spiritual. Ah, this is so hard to explain. This book I've been reading, basically it says that all plants are connected. If you look outside,'—they all dutifully followed my pointed finger out to the wooden deck and beyond, into the garden—'so that bush is actually connected to that one, then that one and so on. Essentially, they are all parts of the same organism.'

'Yes Rosie,' piped up Maisy, speaking with enormous authority for one so young. 'It's the same with groups of human beings. They don't necessarily realize it but they are all connected.' That was the moment in which even the sceptics in the room began to feel the stirrings of an awareness. For some it was a flutter and gone. For others it was a developing curiosity; something they had never before considered and now felt they wanted to, at the very least, learn more.

'Thanks Maisy,' I beamed at my intuitive sister's support. 'We all talk about "such and such has happened in my lifetime". Yet stop and think about it. Since the earth began, this has all been one long lifetime. We are like cells, living and dying as part of the life of this hugely expansive organism. It's my belief and the belief of many others, I might add, that if we can attain a shift through collective consciousness, then the world will respond. Nature will respond. Vibrational energy will change. The world will become a better place.'

HJ spoke up. 'What did Gandhi say? "Be the change you want to see." We know it, we hear it but do we really do it? Are we really listening? Absolutely no! It's like what was said earlier about Einstein, or Pythagoras. We're not listening to all the fantastic advice we've been handed down over the centuries!'

'It's kind of a compelling statement isn't it? I mean, Gandhi's actually demanding something of us. He's insisting we take action,' nodded Adam knowingly.

'Oh, yes,' I continued. 'Gandhi wasn't a sit-around-on-your-backside-and-let's–have-a-nice-talk-about-it kind of guy. He did all sorts of things. He even compelled people to defy British rules, to overflow the jails, to stuff up the system, to show the world that they meant business.'

'Yeah,' agreed Jorge, 'he wasn't a sit-on-your-backside dude, unlike your precious Tibetan monks. I mean, c'mon. What's that all about? Where's the action there, Rosie?' he asked triumphantly.

'Ah Jorge!' I could have strangled him! Tibetan

monks, meditation, it was an age old debate between the two of us. 'I will try to explain for the umpteen-millionth time. They are taking action. Just because in your very limited ideology, it is an action that you don't understand.'

Jorge actually looked a bit crushed.

'I'm not trying to have a go at you. Well maybe I am having a go at constrained cultural thinking. Tibetan Buddhist monks sit literally on top of the world. Lhasa is the most elevated city in the world!'

'And now lots of them, as a result of the Chinese invasion, sit in Dharamshala, in India. And other cities of the world. Now that's a twistory of history,' Jacques added.

'The monks believe their chanting permeates the air, the earth, the vibrational force of the world. Have you heard that deep guttural urrrr, urrrr, urrr?' My really bad monk imitations had everyone laughing.

'Yeah, I've heard it,' said Saurav. 'Sounds demonic, if you ask me.'

I shot him a quick glance. He wasn't helping my cause. 'For people even just hearing the chanting, there is a positive vibrational effect.'

Questions

Discuss the Gandhi quote—'Be the change you want to see in this world.'

- Is there a sense of a call to action?
- Is there a sense of urgency?
- What does it really mean?
- What does it mean for you personally?

Ants in a rainforest are known as a 'keystone species'. It has been suggested that if you remove them all from the forest, essentially you will destroy the forest.

- What do you think would happen if all humans were suddenly removed from the earth? Explore this concept.
- Are we a valuable part of this planet?
- How can we make ourselves a more valued part of our planet?
- What are your own spiritual beliefs and practices? Allow some silent time for people to reflect on this. Then ask people to share.
- We are custodians of the planet. What does the word 'custodian' mean? How do our attitude and actions shift if we perceive ourselves to be custodians of the planet, rather than owners of the planet?

Dessert: Time to Make a Commitment

There are three scripts for Dessert.

Script 1: Attitudes are Shifting

Read the script aloud.

> 'Dessert in the garden,' I proclaimed. 'Everyone follow me.'
>
> The group dutifully picked up dessert bowls, stepped out through the dining room, through the back-porch area and down the steps into the garden. Orlando, the shaggy white dog, happily trotted out alongside everyone. We were met by a delightful scene. Candles bedecked

the garden table, flames flickering and sparkling, mimicking their celestial brothers and sisters in the night sky. A heady aroma wafted our way. Gardenias and jasmine, freshly picked and potted in a central bowl, surrounded by sea shells of intricate form and nature. Maisy's creation. And surrounding us from the garden and fences, a near-summer garden bursting into vibrant passion. The caramelly, sticky date pudding, sat waiting to be served.

An almost full moon shone brightly. The Milky Way creamed its way across the sky.

'How beautiful is the sunlight at night,' breathed HJ, his face glowing as it turned upwards to the moon.

'Moonlight, sweetie,' I corrected. 'You mean how beautiful is the moonlight?'

'Huh?' HJ looked across at me. 'Rosie, a moonlit night is actually a sunlit night. The moon simply reflects the sun's rays. It's not casting its own generated light. This is why we worship the sun. For even in the darkness of night it seeks to light and guide us.'

I bent forward and kissed the top of his forehead. Everyone puddinged to the hilt, we sat back in a balmy October evening.

'Here's something of a phenomenon,' Jacques broke the silence. 'Did you know that the Native Americans and the Indigenous Australians share a particular parable? In both stories an old grandfather sits cross-legged, his grandchildren perched before him keenly listening. Grandpa says quietly: "They ask if a tree falls in a forest and no-one is there to hear it, does it make a sound?

The question is not the sound it may or may not make, my children. The question should be thus: if yet another tree is felled in that forest why isn't anyone listening?"'

A wisp of sorrow swept across us all and passed as quickly as it had come.

'What was that?' whispered Akira.

'Did you feel that too?' Inas whispered back. 'I just suddenly felt so very sad. Was it Jacques' story?'

'Sad. And then as if it was lifted from me,' Akira said.

'Why do you think it lifted?'

'Because people are beginning to listen.'

Questions

Are people beginning to listen? Share stories of the 'good stuff' that is going on out there. Solar-powered cities, roads made of solar panels, banned sale of plastic bottles in San Francisco, winning the logging battles, The Sea Shepherd's winning against the whalers, a music clip that celebrates these things, etc. Show a series of visuals of these achievements. Celebrate them with a toast to the people who have done this, even if we don't know who they are!

Remember, now is the time to shift the conversation to an understanding that very positive things *are* happening, even if we often hear the negative. This derives a sense of hope and therefore more motivation to action.

Script 2. Symbolism and Change

Read the script aloud.

'Symbolism is so important,' said HJ. 'It's what human

beings have responded to throughout the centuries. It's how we interpret art, how we have followed the banners of religions in our millions, it's even how we understand advertising. When Gandhi took on the British Empire, he used a symbolic gesture—the Salt March, a 390 km walk to reclaim a basic right for all Indians to make their own salt. For us today, to win people over in this campaign to save the world, we need a symbol, or perhaps many symbols. We need to find different things that everyone can relate to.'

'So, what you are saying,' said Smita,' is that everyone should support Earth Hour. At the same time every year. For one whole hour, we switch off all electric appliances; all energy-sucking, carbon-polluting gadgets and sit in the dark with our candles burning. The beauty of Earth Hour is not only are we reflecting on our use of energy, but we are doing so alongside millions of people around the world who don't have electricity in their lives anyway. The irony is that whilst we are so constrained by our lack of electricity, sitting there waiting for one hour to pass, those people are still going about their daily business, getting on with it.'

'Let's not get too carried away,' warned Adam, 'I think those people are pretty constrained by their poverty.'

'Yeah, okay, you're right. But the symbolism works all the same. The idea that for one hour, millions of people are sharing in an ultra-positive concept.'

'And besides, how beautiful!' declared Hisashi. 'How beautiful for the world to be unfettered by the buzzing of human-made electrical energy.'

'You're all talking about saving the world from a climate change perspective; asking yourselves what can we do to stop climate change,' spoke up Maisy. 'And that's all well and good. But to me the question is how can we save the world from ourselves? From poverty? From war? From disrespect?'

The group was sitting back, gazing into the night sky, feeling mellow, yet energized and empowered.

'She's right you know. Maisy's right,' HJ explained, 'If we keep delving on the "why", we find we have uncovered a level where the only answer is "it happened due to a lack of love and respect, for nature, and for other peoples."'

Maisy continued, letting her thoughts flow out into the darkness. 'How good would it be to have a War Memorial march, the streets lined with masses of onlookers—people remembering, praying, reflecting, cheering respectfully as empty cars drive slowly and dignified, between them. How cool to have no-one marching, nobody still alive who had actually fought or nursed in a war because we had outlived wars. Here's symbolism for you HJ,' she continued. 'A one-winged dove. The dove symbolizes the peace that we all say we want. But we are merely paying the whole notion lip-service. Its one-wing limits it. No decisive action is taken. It cannot break into flight. That's where we are at. In the world of the one-winged dove.'

'Thou shalt love,' I said out of nowhere and to no-one in particular. 'There are more meanings to be found in the simplicities of life than in a thousand pages of the most complex and gruelling expositions. Thou shalt love,' I repeated. 'I know it sounds too simplistic, but it would work. I'm going to take you all back to my earlier premise.' I sat up straight now, drawing them all into my enthusiasm. 'When you learn to apply the esoteric, things change. Perhaps in the most subtle of ways.'

'But we don't want subtle. We want, no need, dynamic, instant!' barked Jorge. 'We need forceful change and we need it now.'

'Yes. But let's examine the nature of "subtle",' said HJ. 'Are we looking for a quantum leap?'

'Yes, now you've got it.'

'And yet a quantum leap is an electron's state of change, for example, the electron moving from one energy level to another. In actual fact, contrary to the popular usage of the term "quantum leap" the changes of quantum state occur on the submicroscopic level. In other words, they're tinier than tiny. Whilst the leap itself is subtle, the effect may be hugely significant.'

'The Butterfly effect!' interjected Hisashi. 'One small change on one side of the ocean, say the fluttering of a butterfly's wings, can lead to a tsunami on the other side.'

'A subtle change that impacts across the population, can lead to a dynamic effect.' HJ continued, 'We've seen it happen before in India and South Africa. Hey, it happens in a school yard when the dominant kids choose to be friendly and inclusive. The irony is that more often than not people move to a point without fully comprehending "the why" of what they are doing. What was it Spinoza said? "Men are conscious of their own desire but are ignorant of the causes whereby that desire has been determined."'

'And women too.'

'Yes, Rosie, and women too.'

'So, action like saying, "no thanks I don't want your plastic rubbish"; a parent saying no to their child in a toy shop, teaching them they can't have everything; asking the salesgirl at the jewellers, "do you know where your diamonds have come from?"—can be the butterfly effects that lead to tremendous change.'

I was scanning the night sky, searching for inspiration. 'What we need is some magic!'

'Magic? Seriously! Don't go all Harry Potter on us Rosie!' sneered Jorge. 'Personally, I am waiting for the day Harry Potter wakes up in the middle of an asylum and realizes that all the dreadful things his aunt and uncle did to him finally sent him around the twist and that all his so-called magical adventures are purely a form of escapism from his own grim reality!'

'Not that sort of magic, Jorge. Old school alchemy, transformation. In this case, not material items, but attitudes that turn to gold! Do you know what butterflies represent in ancient mythology—Psyche, the goddess who is considered the personification of the soul. The Butterfly effect; quantum transformation of the soul.'

Questions

- Draw a picture of the one-winged dove. What does the world need to do to change this picture? Draw

your answers symbolically around the dove.
- Research what is Earth Hour. Why was it begun? Has it been successful? There is some controversy over Earth Hour. What do we need to consider when we start a project of our own?
- Create and design an act of symbolism that could make a difference in our world. Don't worry about cost or other logistics—there are no limits!
- Quantum leap/The Butterfly effect: give examples of subtle change that can lead to enormous effect.
- Margaret Mead said, 'Never doubt that a small group of thoughtful, committed citizens can change the world. Indeed, it is the only thing that ever has.' Discuss examples. Could this be you?

Script 3. Commitment

Read the script aloud.

> Suddenly I felt like I'd had an epiphany. 'I've been reading de Bono, you know, the guy who invented the Six Hats Theory for Critical Thinking.'
>
> Inas laughed. 'I can never remember which hat is which. My students get it right all the time and they're only nine years old! Anyway, go on Rosie.'
>
> 'Less well-known perhaps but all part of the same theory is his concept of Parallel Thinking. He talks about using it to solve problems, for example, in the board room. Here's the problem, people don't always agree on the same pathway but instead of being adversarial, he invites people to lay down their ideas in parallel, to

reach the very same solution that they are all striving to achieve. I think you can extend the concept well beyond the boardroom, almost in a spiritual sense.'

'It's a solution that is brought about in different ways,' HJ said supportively. 'It means that everyone is working towards the same goal but doing it in their own way. No longer in competition but working symbiotically.'

'Parallel solutions it is!' proclaimed Jorge. All heads turned his way.

'What? I like it,' he said. 'Means I can find my own way. I don't have to take on Rosie's Buddhist chants if I don't want to, and I don't have to become a vegan,' he smiled at Adam. 'But I can still be useful.'

Heads nodded and murmured in approval.

'Right,' Jorge continued, taking the lead now. 'Commitment. Who's doing what?'

'The whole time we've been talking, I've been composing an ad in my head,' said Saurav. 'I'm going to place an advertisement in the *Tokyo Press*. Something along the lines of: "Join me in no longer eating whales, sentient beings of the oceans." Yeah, I'm working on it okay?'

'An ad in that paper will cost you a lot of money!'

'It will cost us a lot more if we don't do something!'

'I'm going to write my letter to Milo,' said Jacques. 'No more plastic hands for advertising, please. And come to think of it, whilst I am at that Sustainable Building conference in Mumbai next month, I will try to approach the government or interest groups as well.'

'Excellent! Sid, Maisy? What about you guys? Can't

have the "children" doing nothing,' I invited.

Sid took a deep breath; he hated the limelight. He had quit drama classes years ago for precisely this reason. 'I'm going to send my photos to BP. Hopefully it will prick their consciences a little. And maybe try to get them in a public gallery. The purpose was to make people think, but I guess if they're just sitting here in our house they're not doing their job.'

'Great idea Sid, and very courageous. Maisy?'

'You know that expression, "The children are our future"? Well that's all very well, but you adults are your own future too, you know! You can't land it all on us. Eighty-year olds still have futures, you know. There's plenty they can do. I don't know if this will work but I'm going to ask Nanna and Pa to do something for my eighteenth birthday.'

'Really, what's that?'

'I'm going to ask them to put solar panels on their roof. I was listening to them talk about it a few weeks back. They were saying that they didn't need solar panels because they could pay their power bills all right and that they wouldn't be around for much longer anyway. They said it was a waste of money. But I think they are missing the point. It's all about legacy. About their grandchildren's future and theirs!'

'Cool idea Maisy. Good luck with that! Adam?'

'I'm championing the vegetarian cause. No more me being the 'Quiet Vegetarian'. I'm joining the Noisy Campaign. Letter writing, placards. It's all happening!'

'Amongst other things, I'm going to meditate and

pray,' I said taking my turn at the dessert 'podium'. 'I know what you're thinking Jorge, but I know this works for me. I'm going to contemplate the ants, cook more pumpkin soup and try to live more simply. And buy that rainwater tank!' I added, glancing at Jacques.

'Most of you know I am doing up my house at the moment.' Akira explained to the group. My commitment, amongst other things,' she added proudly, 'is to use VOC-free paint.' Spotting the curious faces before her, 'Oh, Volatile Organic Compound free paint. You know most paints release chemicals into the air for years after you've painted. These are the clean paints.'

'Mum repaints the walls in a new colour every year,' added Hisashi very seriously. 'My bedroom has recently transformed from blue to chocolate. I can assure you with her extensive use of paint, this would be a very positive outcome. As for me, I will be working on a new form of deriving power from the ocean. To utilize the energy and power of the wave. This will involve several design stages and may take some time to complete even the initial stages of this project. But once completed this will make a significant impact on the future of this world.' Hisashi spoke with the voice and demeanour of a forty-year old. At any other time his statements may have sounded ludicrous or naively arrogant coming from a young child. Yet no one sniggered or passed surreptitious glances because every single person in that garden had faith that this twelve-year old would indeed achieve his goal.

Inas began, 'I'm going to read more; learn more; scan

the internet more. Know more. Then make better choices. Our wedding is only a few weeks away and I, we, still haven't chosen a ring. Not even an engagement ring, let alone a wedding ring. So the idea was to combine the two. Well, I've made a decision tonight. I'm not going to choose a diamond. It's another one of those "traditions" that could have more hidden issues than are immediately apparent to us.'

'Too true,' added HJ.

'Diamonds,' she said, 'where are they coming from? If you are going to choose a diamond at the very least find out its pathway to your finger. So, not for me!'

'Great idea, sweetheart,' said Saurav. He turned to Diana sitting next to him. 'And think of the money we'll save!'

'Sorry, my darling,' Inas challenged, 'I hadn't finished. I prefer sapphires anyway!' Everyone laughed.

'And Diana?'

'Hmmm, been thinking. Sometimes I'm pretty bitchy and moany.'

'And crabby,' I laughed. 'Don't forget crabby.'

'Yes, my good friend. And crabby. You've been talking about subtle change creating great effect. I'm going to start with me. And the way I relate to people.' She looked directly at me and smiled. 'I'm taking up yoga!'

'Yay! Good for you!'

'And I'm making a serious commitment to treating people with more respect. I guess if I treat someone nicely, then they will do the same to the next person.'

'HJ?'

'Me? Well, I'm with Adam.' Adam glanced over at HJ curiously. 'I mean, with the noise campaign. I think we need to get louder. Speak up; be prepared to challenge the big guys. We know what's wrong. We have to have the courage to say it. For me, I'm going to start with the Free Tibet campaign.' He regarded me endearingly. 'I've been listening to you. And thinking about the earth's vibrations. I think we need to place those chanting monks en masse fair and square back on those mountains. I believe the chanting will make a difference to the earth's emotional-spiritual plane.'

'Wow!'

'And I reckon I'm loud enough to yell about a few things at once! So, gay rights will be the go! Equality for all in this country, thanks.'

'Smita, you have the floor.'

'Oh God! Okay. Well, I like everyone's ideas.'

'Well that's just fence-sitting!' threw in Jorge.

Smita glared at him. 'I haven't finished. In fact I hadn't started! I've been listening too. Really listening. I think it's all about attitude. Sometimes it feels like we are moving into a more and more disparate community. If you can treat people badly purely because they don't have as much money as you, we have problems. Wealth, affluence, can be both positive and negative depending on the attitude of the people with the wealth. We have to raise our conscious awareness of not falling into the negative. So, I am going to rise to Rosie's spiritual challenge and see where that takes me.'

Jorge was the last in the group to 'pledge' his intent. 'Somehow we have "othered" ourselves from nature,' he began. 'It shouldn't be man versus nature, yet I think we shouldn't throw away "progress" and completely "go back to nature" either. It has to be humans working with nature. The nurturer becomes the nurtured and vice-versa. I'm going to join the anti-logging campaign. And I'm going to get to work on actively supporting the Conservation Foundation with my money and my hands!'

Questions

It's time to make a commitment. 'Be the change you want to see in this world' is a call to action. Here is a secret that is little known: inside every single one of us is a great idea. We just need to find the key to unlock it. The key usually is covered in a huge healthy dollop of courage. To find the courage sit very still and listen. Think of your strengths, think of your passions. You don't need to do what everyone else is doing or conversely you can find many existing groups who are already galloping with your very same idea. Find one and join them. The most important thing is to take that first step.

Leading scientist and former president of India A.P.J. Abdul Kalam told us: 'You have to dream before your dreams can come true. Everybody has a dream that is achievable. But first you have to have a dream.'

It's time to clearly articulate your dream—then enact it. Give your 'guests'/students some quiet space to think about their commitment. Invite them to write it down. They should then share it—initially in a small group, or to a partner—depending on the size of the group. Tell them—the first step to making a commitment is to say it out loud, to share it with another person. Now, invite people to share their commitment with the whole group, if they wish to. How will you hold yourself to your commitment?

Saying Farewell

Thank everyone for coming. Find a symbolic way to end the dinner party. Again, this will depend on the nature/culture of your guests.

One very good way to end is through a Gratitude ceremony. This can take place in various ways. For example, people stand in a circle, each person holding incense sticks or Chinese joss sticks. Light the incense/joss sticks and on the count of three everyone spins outwards, waves the sticks gently and says to themselves three things they are grateful for, then three wishes for the planet, then the first step they are going to take—*their commitment to our planet.*

Join The Gandhi Experiment's campaign to get the good stuff out through social media. Whilst still facing up to the tough stuff that needs to be done, flood our teenagers' minds with hope! http://www.thegandhiexperiment.com/free-lessons-for-teachers-and-parents/

Create your own 'positivity wall' in your classroom/at home—encourage students to add images and stories to the wall frequently.

Two

The Best Forgiveness Role-Play Ever

Forgiveness is the attribute of the strong.

GANDHI

I LOVE stories about Gandhi because I think they demonstrate that whether we are politicians, journalists, teachers, parents, or salespeople, our everyday actions and decisions are what will set the scene for our relationships in our family, our classrooms and even within our government. They also remind us we have a choice, to think differently; to choose another response to the one we might quickly leap to. Here is one such story.

One day Gandhi was travelling on a train across India. As he boarded the train one of his shoes slipped from his foot. It fell on to the tracks. The train began its journey, Gandhi calmly removed his other shoe and threw it towards its partner. People were surprised by this action and someone asked, 'Why did you do that?' Gandhi answered, 'Well now when someone finds them, they will have a pair of shoes.'

If we can plant the simplest acts of thought and kindness at our core, we will bring these to the tables of our family, of our workplace, of our legal mediators, and of our political forums.

One of the most powerful books I have ever read on brutal racism—Harper Lee's *To Kill a Mockingbird*—is told through the eyes of an innocent child. The book teaches us 'to walk in someone else's shoes', to understand their lives, to gain empathy. We can do so then 'return' to our own lives to apply the learning. Furthermore, like Gandhi, we can also 'give' our own 'shoes' and allow 'the other' to walk with more comfort and dignity. It puts a smile on my face to think that somebody probably did find those shoes lying on the railway tracks, and spent their days literally walking in Gandhi's shoes without ever knowing!

Gandhi employed lateral ways of approaching a problem time and time again. It's a kind of creativity. Einstein told us, 'We cannot solve our problems with the same thinking that we used to create them.' The creativity is dependent upon the ability to empathize. To put yourself in someone else's shoes and ask, 'What if that was me?' Or, with even more honesty, 'Hang on, that has been me.'

By now I can hear you asking, 'Isn't the title of this chapter, The Best Forgiveness Role-Play Ever? What does this Gandhi shoe story have to do with forgiveness?'

You see, the role-play you are about to participate in is about forgiveness, but it is also about something that runs as a theme through this entire book—the ability to think differently and therefore react or respond differently, and to empathize.

First, let us examine the concept of forgiving. When was the last time you forgave someone for something? Was the forgiving, itself, a challenging and difficult thing to do? We are forever telling children to 'say you're sorry.' Yet as adults we can find this same act almost impossible. What is it that gets in the way—that almost literally stands as a separately, newly-created entity, between two people, blocking their ability to communicate?

What is forgiveness? It perhaps means different things to different people. Maybe for me, in certain cases, I have managed to 'reconcile', rather than forgive. Has everyone I have ever done wrong to, managed to forgive me? I don't know for sure, but I seriously doubt it. Whatever your definition, wherever you feel you fit in these scenarios, the questions themselves are certainly worth considering.

I recall sharing a deeply personal story with a woman who listened intently then spoke quietly. 'Have you forgiven them?' It threw me. She continued, 'I'm a Christian. I want you to ask yourself this—if Jesus could forgive those who crucified him, why can't you forgive these two?' Boy, she was making me squirm. So often in my classes with secondary students I have pointed out to them, 'If Nelson Mandela could walk out of jail after twenty-seven years and forgive those who held him imprisoned, then it is living proof that we are also capable of forgiving anyone.' No-one, least of all me, is saying that forgiveness is easy.

Forgiveness does not solely belong to, nor is it owned by, the religions. We often view concepts such as forgiveness, hope and peace as religious constructs. Sometimes we even shy away from them because we don't like to be 'preached at' or suffer what we perceive to be religious dogma. Yet forgiveness—the ability to forgive and to accept being forgiven—is one of the most needed and powerful ways for us to move forward, as individuals, and as a collective.

In November 2014, I was travelling across India, running The Gandhi Experiment workshops in schools, when one evening, casually browsing on Facebook, I came across a photo and story that a friend had posted: 'The Babemba tribe'. I was completely taken by the extraordinary lateral thinking of this Southern African tribe in regards to what they do when someone in their tribe does something harmful or shameful. By the very next day I had turned this into a role-play and trialled it on a group of young students in Pune.

Since then using this role-play I have facilitated The Best Forgiveness Role-Play Ever (the title is a bold claim, I know!) in India, Pakistan, Indonesia and Melbourne, Australia, at primary, secondary, university level, for students and for teachers. This has fast become an impactful role-play. Both adults and students immediately 'get it'. They understand its power and resonance for their own context.

LESSON PLAN

At school or in a forum with students or adults/At home (see notes following the role-play)

As the facilitator, you are standing in front of the participants and are about to guide them through a role-play. You need to be very engaging, draw them into the story; weave and craft it for them. Everything in quotation marks—that's you speaking. Show this photo of the Babemba tribe. Leave it up on the screen overseeing the role-play.

The Best Forgiveness Role-Play Ever • 47

The Babemba Tribe
Photo credit: Jessica Hilltout: From her project AMEN
Abukari from Kpenjipei in Northern Ghana

Read this passage aloud:[2]

> In the Babemba tribe in Africa, when a person acts irresponsibly or unjustly, he/she is placed in the centre of the village, alone and unfettered. All work ceases, and every man, woman and child in the village gathers in a large circle around the 'accused' individual. They remain there, surrounding this person, for two to three days.

Now start the discussion.

> So, let's say this person has stolen a lot of food. This has impacted the whole community. If we imagine we (the

---

[2] Zunin, Leonard MD, Zunin, Natalie (1972), *Contact: The First Four Minutes*. Ballantine Books, Random House: New York

> entire audience) are that tribe—it has impacted us—and all our children, family and friends.

Allow the profound effect this would have on the tribe to settle over participants.

> The offender has been found and has been brought to the centre of the village. All the people of the tribe now surround this 'criminal'—for two to three days. What do you think is the most likely thing that will happen next?

Let that question sit, allow people to imagine. Next say:

> I'm going to invite someone to come up to the front and 'be' the offender—be the person who has stolen the food. And now we need six people to surround this person in a semicircle (so the audience can see). These six people are members of the village.

Help set up this situation, with the offender in clear view of the audience.

> So, what do you think might now happen to this person who has stolen the food?

Encourage lots of answers, both from the six people in the semicircle and the broader audience. Typical responses include:

- they will beat him/her up;
- they will yell abuses and throw things at him/her;
- they will exile him/her, banish them from the tribe;
- they might chop off his/her hand to show this person is a thief;
- they might even kill him/her.

Remind people that 'through history and even now currently in the world, these exact same punishments have actually occurred for similar offences. Examples of "shaming" someone who has committed a crime have included shaving their head, holding signs that proclaim the crime, making them kneel on broken glass, throwing things at them, beating, flogging, death.'

Now say, 'So, here we are. The offender has been caught and is now surrounded.' Pause, then read this poignant progression[3]:

> In the Babemba tribe when someone commits a wrongful act, that person will be taken to the centre of the village. For two to three days the tribe will surround them... Then each person in the tribe speaks to the accused, one at a time, about all the good things the person in the centre of the circle has done in his/her lifetime.

Pause, let this sink in, repeat, 'They will be told every good thing they have ever done, every strength, every kindness—all their positive attributes. So, let's try it. Let's now tell him/her all the good things they have done for us.' Invite the six participants in the semicircle, role-playing the tribes-people, to join in. You lead with an example, looking directly at the person in the centre.

> I remember when the village was short of water. You walked for miles to another well to help bring water back to us all.

---

[3]Zunin, Leonard MD, Zunin, Natalie (1972), *Contact: The First Four Minutes*. Ballantine Books, Random House: New York.

Invite the others to add their stories. It doesn't matter what order, or if someone cannot think of one, move on and then come back to them. If they run out of things to say, invite the audience to join in. This broadens the reach and allows more people to express and therefore *feel* the effect.

Typical examples have been:

- I remember when you helped gather firewood with the kids.
- You helped my sister with her homework when she was struggling.
- When my mother was ill you sat by her when I couldn't.
- You have this great smile and it always makes me smile.
- You walked for miles every day to get us water when the water in our well dried up.

If the group runs out of examples add another one of your own, or invite an audience member to continue. This gives those up at the front time to think.

When the 'tribespeople' have finished giving their affirmations, stop everything. Then quietly yet firmly, ask the offender to describe how he/she is feeling. 'How are you feeling? What are you thinking when you hear all this said about you?'

Allow the offender to talk freely. Encourage them to keep talking. What you will see is a very genuine response, even though this is only a role-play, because you have reached their hearts.

Typical responses have included:

- I feel overwhelmed.
- I feel loved.
- I feel ashamed that I have done something to my wonderful friends.
- These people really like me!
- I feel genuinely repentant.
- I want to make up for what I have done.

Now share with them:

> Child psychologists tell us that one of the most important things children need to feel is a sense of belonging. It is therefore incumbent on us as friends/educators/parents to ensure each child feels they belong. Tell me, what happens when someone is ostracized? What would happen if we had kicked him/her (pointing to the offender) out of the village?

Typical responses have included:

- He would seek revenge.
- She would return to steal more—do something else.
- Hate grows within.
- He might even commit suicide because he feels so shunned by his group/his community/his family.

Ask, 'What would happen if we banished another offender, and yet another.'

Typical response:

- We would create an enemy of our tribe.

Allow this discussion to flow for a short while. Then ask:

So what now is the likely difference in outcome if this person has been told that essentially they are a good person? What difference does it make when we do something wrong and yet we still feel included? What course do you think our actions will take?

Turn to the offender. 'What do you think you might now do about having stolen the food?'

Typical responses:

- I'll find a way to make up for it.
- I will appreciate all my family and friends even more.
- I'll work really hard to restore their faith in me.

State:

> The manner in which the Babemba tribe handles this situation allows for forgiveness and reconciliation to follow. The 'offender' is held accountable, yet is not labelled, nor judged. Guilt and shame are not lorded over them. They do not have to spend the rest of their lives backed into a corner. Can anyone see how this might have longer positive gain for the individual and for community building?

The real learning comes with the following statement, the beliefs which underpin the entire community's action[4]:

> The tribe recognizes that the correction for non-integrous behaviour is not punishment, but love and the

---

[4] Sheryl "Shera" Sever, Igniting the SparkTM, www.sherylsever.com http://sherylsever.com/2007/11/know-your-song-and-sing-it/)

remembrance of identity. They believe a friend, a coach or teacher is someone who knows your song and sings it to you when you have forgotten it. They are not fooled by the mistakes you have made or the dark images you hold about yourself. They remember your beauty when you feel ugly; your wholeness when you are broken; your innocence when you feel guilty; and your purpose when you are confused.

I usually repeat this phrase because it is so powerful and beautiful, 'Someone who knows your song and sings it to you when you have forgotten it.' I find even the youngest children resonate with this statement and you can feel an energy shift in the room.

How do we apply this learning to our lives?

Here comes the crux of the activity. When all the participants of the role-play—especially the 'offender'—have been thanked, heartily applauded and have sat down, ask the next question.

'How can we apply this learning in our schools and in our homes?'

It is very important to have the time for this step. It is one thing to perform the role-play and leave people thinking, 'ah that was interesting', 'that was different' but the real learning/change-making comes from application.

Remind them that 'we are not the Babemba tribe. We live in differently constructed societies. Without taking someone to the centre of the village how can we apply the essence of their forgiveness ritual?'

'Having seen the power of, and understood the long-term

impact of this lateral approach to forgiving, how can we apply this in our schools and in our homes?'

Allow some quiet time for people to pen their thoughts. Perhaps five minutes. Share their responses and allow exploration of some of these ideas. Some typical responses from adult workshops have been:

- I can see how this could work for kids fooling around in class or in the schoolyard.
- This would be good for kids with friendship issues. When one kid has done something to a whole group of friends, remind them of the strength of their friendship before trying to unravel the problem.
- I can see how this would help a student 'feel something' about what they have done and not just pay lip service to saying sorry.
- When writing reports, we can always start with the good things about the student, then move to the need for improvement, and then finish with more good things.
- When a child at school has done something quite inappropriate, I have often begun the conversation with, 'You aren't usually like this. You're actually a really good person. What's going on with you that has brought this behaviour?'

It reminds us, as teachers and parents to get to the root of the problem so that we don't become immediately reactive and find ourselves meting out an undeserving punishment—only to discover later, that our own actions will warrant forgiveness from the child or student! Give more time for people to write down others' suggestions and develop their own ideas.

Then ask: 'What is the first step you will take to ensure this takes place?'

I was once at a workshop where it was suggested by someone that this very same Babemba strategy could take place in front of an entire school assembly. The idea was immediately discredited by the teachers sitting in that same audience. They could see, through their experiences, that this may well become a public shaming and have the opposite of the desired outcome. In the schools I have taught in, I would tend to agree.

However, the idea of sharing someone's positive points, their strengths, does indeed work with a small group of students—possibly a friendship group—who are suffering instances of bullying from within the group. Remember, this is not about excusing the person's behaviour. Nor is it about removing consequences. The consequences may be different and the long-term outcomes far more forgiving and inclusive.

As a teacher or parent you need to use your insight and discretion to make decisions about how to apply this technique.

Performing The Best Forgiveness Role-Play Ever allows students (and adults) to learn the lesson, to discuss and explore the concepts of forgiveness, inclusion/exclusion, bullying, reconciliation and empathy without pinpointing someone as an actual example. Because it is a kinaesthetic activity, the learning is 'felt' and therefore further enhanced and embedded. Furthermore, because the Babemba tribe teaches us such a lateral approach, it helps us to think differently, to re-wire our brains to less reactive responses and to seek alternative solutions.

How Do We Forgive Ourselves?

Sometimes forgiving ourselves can be the hardest thing—even more difficult than forgiving a friend or family member. The process of forgiving ourselves can be fundamental in helping us to forgive others. To forgive yourself, practise this exercise, using the learning from The Best Forgiveness Role-Play Ever.

Say to the group: 'Shut your eyes and recall a time when it has been difficult to forgive yourself. Now take yourself to the centre of "your village". Tell yourself all the good things you have done. You may hear the voices of others, family, friends, even of those you may have hurt. But they are naming the good things about you. Telling you the good stuff about the person you really are. Open your eyes and write three good things about yourself.'

'Now one more good thing.'

'And now one more.'

'Tell yourself that you know essentially you are a good person.'

Ask the group this question: 'What courageous step will you take to try to rectify the situation?'

At Home

We can use The Best Forgiveness Role-Play Ever as parents in our homes with our own children (or even with our partner). Perhaps rather than 'act out' the role-play, you can talk through the story with your children—still inviting the same responses—'What would you do to the offender? How would you feel if…' And come to the same point of realization on the power of love and inclusivity over shame, fear and exclusion. The idea is to remind ourselves to deal with the child's behaviour rather than allowing the child to feel they are their behaviour.

A Cute Story with a Lateral Approach

My cousin's daughter has two young children. When they get cross and upset with each other and the squabbling begins, she takes them outside and asks them to hold hands. She then leaves them to sit whilst holding hands until they have sorted it out. Invariably they decide that they actually love each other and say sorry of their own volition.

Photo credit: April Cameron 'Time Out'

In Conclusion

I am not suggesting that this method is the be-all and end-all pathway to forgiveness.

What I do know, however, is that The Best Forgiveness Role-Play Ever has a powerful impact in helping people to think differently. It draws out people's compassionate and emotional responses to tough situations. It allows for all involved to move forward. Above all, we often recognize ourselves as having been that offender in the centre of the group. We would hope and pray that people are able to forgive us and see beyond our actions at that point in time.

I know and understand the power of positive human energy. Peace and forgiveness are teachable!

The Best Forgiveness Role-Play Ever has enormous benefits when role-played with student and adult groups. Contact me to visit your school or community forum. The Gandhi Experiment is also now running teacher workshops and parent seminars. Visit www.thegandhiexperiment.com

Three

The Utopian Scale

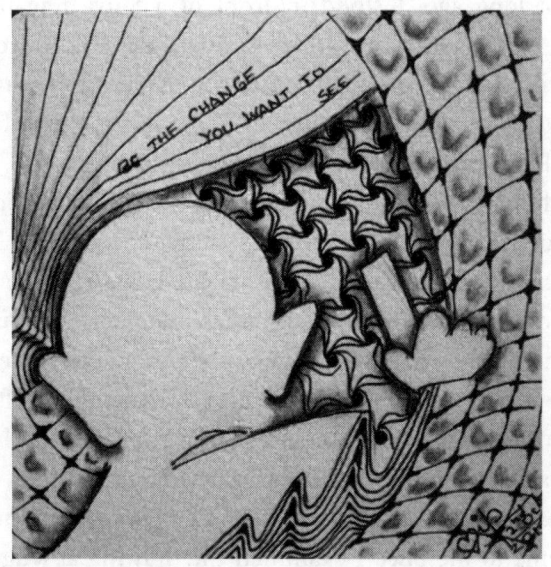

'The Utopian Scale can shift perspective.'

WHEN I first gained the courage to say out loud, 'I believe we can achieve World Peace' (and I can assure you I am no Miss Universe contestant) there were people who shook their heads in disbelief at me, 'It can't be done.' There were even people who laughed and derided the idea. Fortunately for me, I was able to recall Gandhi's words: 'First they ignore you, then they laugh at you, then they fight you, then you win.'

What is The Utopian Scale? And what is its relevance to the concept of world peace? For everything in this world, we are all on a scale—the autism scale, the IQ scale, the obsessive-compulsive scale, the sexual preference scale. And, whether we know it or not, we are all on The Utopian Scale. The Utopian Scale is a scale of attitude towards the possibilities of peace.

Not long ago, I stood in front of a Shiva lingam, at a Hindu temple on a busy road in Suva, Fiji. I stood quietly, very still, eyes closed. And a message came: 'Some say hope is futile. This is not the futility of hope; this is the fertility of hope.' Plant the seeds and watch hope grow.

Before we explore the activity below—The Utopian Scale—I want to share with you how the picture, above, came to me, and what it meant for me. My friend Dilip Patel is a very talented man—an engineer and a facilitator in 'Life Purpose' workshops. But what I didn't know about him, until recently, is that he is also an artist, in particular, a 'Zentangle craftsman.' For my birthday Dilip sent me this picture that he himself had drawn—Gandhi, staff in hand, striding mindfully ahead. Needless to say, I was thrilled. Here are the rambling thoughts that came to me once I examined the drawing at length.

There is so much happening in this drawing—so much movement—Gandhi in action! It seems to me that Gandhi is drawing back the veil of illusion. The illusion is what most of us kid ourselves about, the materialistic world. Our reality of what we believe we 'need' to be 'successful' in life, can alter immediately simply by being brave enough to draw back the veil, and see our landscape in a new light. Gandhi told us, 'We feel all the freer and lighter for having cast off the tinsel of civilization.'[5] Now here's an experiment for you: try thinking of living with a little less of the materialistic stuff that surrounds us and see how it feels. Notice the difference—do you feel lighter? Why is that?

And what of this powerful Gandhi statement; 'The world has enough for everyone's need, but not enough for everyone's greed.' In her exposé on the relevance of Gandhi's practice to current economic models, journalist Rajni Bakshi writes, 'Nobody should be asked to pay the price for the majority to benefit.'[6] What do you think she means by that? When I founded The Gandhi Experiment as a social enterprise, I had to ask myself some deep introspective questions, including this—what was my personal relationship with money? As a citizen of a first world nation, living in Melbourne, Australia, a city filled with undeniably wonderful benefits, yet coupled with expensive living costs, in particular, the cost of housing, how would I choose to live?

Gandhi literally cast off the tinsel. In memorials to Gandhi we can view photographs of the progression, the metamorphosis from conventional lawyer to barely-clad sage. It is quite a stunning visual transformation and I am quite sure Gandhi was well aware of the impact. Likewise, when you visit Gandhi Smriti in Delhi, we are shown his array of

---

[5] Excerpts taken from, Fischer L., (1983), Ed., *The Essential Gandhi: An Anthology of His Writings on His Life, Work, and Ideas*, p. 47, Vintage Spiritual Classics, Random House: New York.
[6] *The Guardian*, January 2013

accumulated possessions. All that Gandhi owned sits in one small exhibit. It is meagre to say the least. His eyeglasses, a cup, a fork, a bowl and a pair of sandals...less than ten items in all. I want to note here that every bit of living like that was a choice; his conscious choice.

Should I try to emulate his life? Or is my role to spread his message of non-violence? Of peace? I mean, I didn't have to live like him...did I? But to try capture his message, his essence, should I renounce all my material possessions? Should I live in poverty? How would I raise my children? The fear, the doubts, set in. I am a single mother and as much as my children are supported by their father, and by what they, as young adults, contribute, I feel I needed to remain a part of their financial equation. Did Gandhi get his relationship with his children right?

I struggled for a long time to resolve these questions; this was a very real dilemma for me. Until one day I had a clear resolution. I like to see it as a small epiphany. Why would I wish to live in poverty when one of my clear goals is to eradicate poverty? I don't wish to see anyone on this planet living in such a subjugated position, so logically why would I choose to inflict this on myself? And then this, another small epiphany: Was Gandhi living in poverty? Or was he living in simplicity?

At the top of Dilip's drawing is another famous Gandhi quote—perhaps the most well-known of his mantras. 'Be the change you want to see' is echoing louder and louder— reverberating across the land. If I am to be the change—and part of the change is that no-one lives in poverty—then nor should I. In fact I don't want to live at either extreme, not poverty, nor opulence. My decision? I would live in the realm of *enough*. I would live in *enough* and provide *enough* for my children. Or, to clarify: in terms of materialistic things, I would live in *enough*, in terms of spirituality, I would live in abundance.

Looking back on my life now, I think I began my earthly journey in a state of 'What is best for me?' Now I find myself asking, on a daily basis, 'What is best for the community? For us all?' The irony is, as it turns out, that what is best for all, is best for me! Bakshi tells us, 'Gandhi visualizes a very creative dynamics between the individual and collective well-being. He sees the two as being in sync.'[7]

At this point, I am quite sure some of you are saying, 'Hang on, that quote about *be the change*, that's not exactly what Gandhi said. That's a misquote. Somebody else tagged that phrase.' Yes, you would be right and we don't even know that person's name. In fact what Gandhi did say was this: 'If we could change ourselves, the tendencies in the world would also change…We need not wait to see what others do.' Personally, I applaud the fact that somebody has taken the essence of this message and tagged it to a memorable mantra.

You see, so often we attribute all the 'good quotes' and all the 'good deeds' to a handful of people in this world. When I travel, I often ask people to name the world's role models. Who are the peacemakers? No matter which country, they all name the same few. Invariably they include Gandhi, Martin Luther King, Nelson Mandela and Mother Theresa, and of course religious leaders—Jesus, Prophet Mohammed (SAWS), and the Buddha. Then one day, a lady in Fiji said to me, 'We need to add in "You and Me".'

---

[7] Ibid.

64 • *The Gandhi Experiment*

So, a quiz question for you. Who said, 'Pray—using your soul's light and let each prayer be a light for others.' Don't know? You give up? Actually, it was my friend, Susan Stewart. You see, we all have such talents. And to really enact positive change in our world, we need to recognize and activate our own talents. Remember, Nelson Mandela told us, 'We all need to step up beyond our own expectations of ourselves.' It reminds me of a time I was running The Gandhi Experiment workshop in Melbourne with a particularly young group, ten-year olds, Year 4 students. We were unpacking this question: 'What does it mean when we say that we don't *own* the planet, but are *custodians* of this planet?' After sharing their thoughts, one of these ten-year olds looked up at me and said, 'We need millions and millions of custodians across this planet.' I asked him if he could become the prime minister of our country! In our drawing, Gandhi is handing out his staffs, passing on his mantle, to many, including this young boy.

Look carefully again at the drawing. Gandhi's body is fluttering like the leaves of a favourite, well-read book. An appropriate metaphor given that Gandhi tried as much as possible to live his life as an open book. 'My life is my message,' he said.

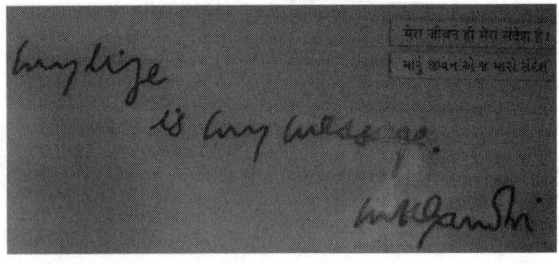

Photo credit: Margaret Hepworth from the Sabarmati Ashram, Ahmedabad.

'Be the change you want to see in the world.' For so long I focused on *'the change'*. What is the change I want to see? Then whilst writing my speech as a guest speaker for the launch of the Afghan Australian Initiative, in Melbourne, the word *'Be'* suddenly became emboldened. *'Be* the change'—It's a command, an imperative. Do it, be it, live it, step up-now!

'*As a man changes his own nature, so does the attitude of the world change towards him.*' (Gandhi)

'*Changing one's relationship with the world may be the key to a harmonious, loving existence.*' (My friend Bernadette Hugh-Clink)

Pick up one of Gandhi's staffs and let's walk towards The Utopian Scale, which begins with a question, 'Do you believe in world peace?' followed by, 'Where are *you* on The Utopian Scale? How does your attitude, or what you choose to believe, contribute to the *possibility* of world peace?'

LESSON PLAN

Draw a line across the board or, if you are teaching a smaller group or working from home, across the landscape of a piece of paper. One single line. Mark the two ends 0 and 10. Now write these words boldly above the line:

The Utopian Scale
0 ——————————————————————— 10

Ask each person in turn, 'Do you believe in the concept of world peace? That this is something the world wants, or should be aiming for?'

Then: 'If your answer is a complete and utter no, you would

place a mark on The Utopian Scale at 0. If your answer is a complete and utter yes, then place your mark at 10. Or your answer may be somewhere in between.'

If you are facilitating a larger group, you may ask them to complete the task on their own paper. Then invite 10–20 people to come up and place their mark on the board. Invite the group not to over think the question; 'A "gut response" is what we are looking for.'

Second question: 'Do you believe we can *achieve* world peace?' This time use a different coloured marker to place the responses. Again, no at 0, yes at 10. If you believe we can achieve a measure of world peace, then place your mark somewhere correspondingly along the scale. Now step back, take a look at your Utopian Scale and where people's answers sit. Then open to discussion.

'Does anyone have any questions/observations on this?'

Typical responses include—what is world peace? An end to violence and conflict? An end to inner violence/inner conflict? Being able to forgive others? To forgive yourself? Who do you mean when you say 'we'? Do you mean us here in this room? Do you mean all humans across the world?

In particular, note this observation of the scale—is there a gap between people's beliefs in world peace as a concept and the belief that world peace can be achieved? Why would that be? Discuss this.

Now go back to the scale and write these two words. At 0 write the word 'Dystopia.' At 10 write the word 'Utopia.'

Dystopia 0 ——————————————— Utopia 10

What do 'dystopia' and 'utopia' mean? Here are the dictionary definitions:

> Dystopia: *a society characterized by human misery, such as squalor, oppression, disease, and overcrowding*
> Utopia: *an ideal place or state; any visionary system of political or social perfection*
> (http://dictionary.reference).

But we can be far more creative than that. We want to capture the essence and connotations of these words. Allow three minutes quiet time for students to write—in prose or words and phrases, sketch, and/or imagine what dystopia and utopia look like, feel like, sound like. Share some answers. Are there places in the world now that match these definitions?

To explore the concept of utopia further, ask this question: If India (replace with the country you are currently in) was the best country it could be, what would it:

- Look like?
- Feel like?
- Smell like?
- Sound like?

Allow time for students to answer this, then share as a group.

Next tell them to think about India (or your country) in its current state and answer the following:

- If India was a musical instrument, what musical instrument would it be?
- If India was a piece of furniture, what piece of furniture would it be?

- If India was a vehicle, what vehicle would it be?
- If India was a mural, what story would it tell?
- Now, what story would you want it to tell your grandchildren?

Go back to the scale. Where is the world right now? Closer to dystopia or utopia?

(Please send your group's results to me at margaret@margarethepworth.com—telling me where you are from, where the discussion took place, age group, etc. so we can begin to compile a 'world perception'.)

Lead a discussion that begins: 'Now we are entering the realms of imagination, moving away from the confined and the blinkered, to a *place of possibility*.'

Ask: 'What was the first thing that Wilbur and Orville Wright had in order to achieve the flight? What did the suffragettes have when they campaigned for women's right to vote? What has every inventor had that has led to the eventual success of his or her invention?'

The belief that it could be done!

The belief that 'it is possible' will pull the mainstream in that direction. So that whether or not we reach a utopia, we will sit so much closer to it.

Teacher's note: It will come as no surprise to anyone, that the latest research tells us that when faced with an all-consuming sense of fear, dread and hopelessness, young people will throw up their hands, shrug their shoulders and move to a state of apathy and despair. 'What's the use, it's all over anyway.' This can lead to any number of other issues including binge drinking, drugs, depression and violence.

The recently termed scientific study, positive psychology, has been defined as the study of the strengths and virtues that enable individuals, communities and organizations to thrive (www.positivepsychologyinstitute.com.au). Most notably, positive psychology has proven that by working on our personal growth, including our signature strengths, we move towards optimism. And in moving to optimism, we tend to do more, create more, 'be more'. Positive psychology in practice has even been shown to be an intervention to mental illness, such as depression.

Whilst maintaining a realistic view of the more negative events unfolding in the world, if teenagers are also presented with the amazing things people are doing to help find solutions to these global issues, something remarkable happens. I have seen this many, many times with my own eyes. Teenagers become the most altruistic people on the planet. They want to help; they want to do more. Flood them with a sense of hope and they will do that 'more' in leaps and bounds.

Discuss: 'If every person in the world completely and wholeheartedly believed world peace was possible, and took immediate action towards it, we could achieve it by today. You can now choose to be cynical and sneer, "As if this is going to happen!" Or, you can choose to stop, and sense the wonder of it. And agree that it is possible. Some of you will be able to believe this now, right now. If you can't believe something of this scale, just yet, then what smaller part of it can you believe, as a first step? The belief that it is possible will pull the mainstream in that direction.'

Next, share this story:

> One particular evening at my meditation group, we were deep in a guided meditation. I could still hear the voice of our meditation group mentor, Bernadette, wafting across the room. In that state, it is a voice that has no physical presence any more, it just simply is a voice, a voice of guidance. You can choose to follow this voice or wander off on your own path. All is good. Bernadette had taken us on a small journey and now I heard her voice quietly say, 'You are floating, higher and higher…into space. You are leaving Earth to go to a beautiful planet, the most beautiful planet you have ever seen.'

Stop the story here to ask the students: 'Where would you have gone? What do you envisage when you see the "most beautiful planet you have ever seen"?'

Continue the story:

> My inner consciousness was drifting through space, willingly seeking out this glorious planet. Floating higher and higher, I began my journey upwards, completely engulfed by the experience. Until suddenly, I stopped. Mid-air, mid-space. Completely of its own volition, my body turned and faced Earth. And this is what I saw.
>
> Stunningly beautiful, glowing within its own aura, a planet in harmony—Earth as it could look if we allowed it to be. I had found the 'most beautiful planet'; it was our planet, Earth. This thought came and settled over me: I have witnessed world peace.

Invite student responses to this story. 'Were you expecting the Earth to be the most beautiful planet? Why? Why not?

How do we help make our world the most beautiful planet?'

Now go back to The Utopian Scale on your board and take one last very important step. Draw a new line on the board, with no numbers, just one straight line. Write the word 'dystopia' at one end and, repeat the word 'dystopia,' at the other end. Write 'utopia' in the centre. 'We have now shifted perception. We no longer need to see utopia as an extreme. Dystopia is the extreme, while utopia is the grounded, very real centre.'

Please share your class' responses to The Utopian Scale with me at margaret@margarethepworth.com. I would love to hear your students' thoughts and observations as well as yours as the parent or teacher, of course. We would like to compile a 'worldly perception' firstly half way through this activity and again at the conclusion of The Utopian Scale activity.

Four

Einstein's Theory of Why? Why? Why?

GETTING TO THE ROOT CAUSE OF THE PROBLEM

'Change begins with me.' Well why does it begin with me? Why can't it begin with someone else? What would Gandhi have said in response to that question?

This chapter is all about the 'Whys?' It is by asking why that we get to the all-important root cause of a problem. In doing so, we may be able to alter our perception of the issue at hand.

It is a commonly held view that Albert Einstein was a genius. The crazy-haired scientist of the 1950s developed the theory of relativity, resulting in that famous equation $e=mc^2$. Yet Einstein himself stated he was not a genius; what he had was innate curiosity. He explained that when he found the answer to a scientific problem, whereas most of us would say, 'I found it!' and stop the search right there, Einstein would pause, allow a moment of inner applause, and then ask, 'But why is that?' And when he subsequently came to the end of the next question chain, producing a deeper answer to the original question, again he would pause, smile and ask, 'And why is that?' In a sense he never lost that child-like drive to keep asking 'Why? Why? Why?'

In recognizing the depths to where this took Einstein, I developed an educational tool, naming it Einstein's Theory of Why? Why? Why? In inviting our teenagers, indeed ourselves, to consider a person's behaviour, a situation, a current or historical event and continue to ask, 'Why? Why? Why?' they will unearth the root cause of what is going on. This, in turn, as it did for Albert Einstein, will lead to a deeper point of understanding. True education is all about understanding.

We can use Einstein's Theory of Why? Why? Why? in many and varied situations. Some of the following activities are for use in our classrooms and at home, with our teenagers. Some of them, as you will see, are for us, as adults to use with ourselves, or teachers with other teachers, or parents together. They are designed to help us become better teachers and more understanding parents. Specific examples have been used; you will be able to supplant other examples that you feel are more relevant to your class or context, still applying the same methodology. You will find more examples explored in the video-clips: www.thegandhiexperiment.com

Once we understand the root cause of the problem, we can apply more relevant steps forward to resolve the issue than the one we have perhaps been using. We are equipping our teenagers with lifelong strategies to be able to unravel conflict, often before it grows into deeper and more problematic tensions. Interestingly, the Gandhian principle, 'Change begins with me,' when combined with the 'Why? Why? Why?' chains, can bring about transformative change.

LESSON PLAN

Here are five ways we can apply Einstein's Theory of Why? Why? Why? at school or at home. Each time we are aiming to get to the root cause of the issue at hand.

A: Unravelling Behaviour

- Invite your students to sit in pairs.
- Ask them to think of a person outside of the classroom/school, who they often feel very annoyed by or they have problems getting on with, particularly if they have never been able to understand what the problem is. This could be, for example, a cousin, aunt or uncle. Or someone else who is not a relation, e.g. a shopkeeper in a shop they often frequent, who is always rude and abrupt.
- They share the story with their partner, describing the issue rather than the person.
- As they share, their partner needs to intervene often with, 'Why do you think that person does that?'
- The partner continues to ask Why? Why? Why? until the person telling the story comes to a new point of understanding about the situation, and has a 'light-bulb' moment. 'Oh I'd never considered that...' For example, sometimes we realize that someone is going through a very difficult time in a personal relationship. It is affecting their outward behaviour to others. In a sense, this doesn't excuse their rudeness, however, it most certainly helps explain it and this may help soften our attitude and our ability not to be rude back.

Teacher's note: Here are some light-bulb moments that have occurred for teachers following this approach when sharing behaviour of children in their classroom. The results I have given here may look obvious but in actual fact they took a while to derive at by following the process and continuing to strive to get to the bottom of the issue. Sometimes what seems so obvious is marred by our quick reaction to someone's behaviour.

Question: 'Why is she arrogant? Such a rude person.'

Root cause: She was taught or raised to be arrogant.

Looking to a solution: How might we help her change her behaviour to be better accepted by her peers, so they don't continue to moan about her behind her back?

Question: 'Why does he play up in such an annoying and distracting way?'

Root cause: He is suffering from bi-polar disorder.

Looking to a solution: How can we provide a pathway to professional help?

Question: 'Why can't she sit still in my classroom? Agh—I'm going to MAKE her sit still.'

Root cause: She has a learning disability—an audio-processing issue—that has never been diagnosed.

Looking to a solution: How might I change my teaching style and work with her parents to accommodate this so she (and others like her in my class) can learn better?

Question: 'Why is he late to class again? It's so frustrating and interrupts my lesson!'

Root cause: He has problems at home. His parents are not supporting his schooling.

Looking to a solution: How can we talk about this and support him rather than punish him?

Question: 'Why is that kid "stuffing around" in my classroom and not doing his work? He's so lazy!'

Root cause: He is vision-impaired and cannot even see the board properly, but we never knew that. (A comment on this: a friend of mine once told me she thought it normal that when she travelled home from school on a tram, everything outside of the tram was a blur. It wasn't until finally her eyes were tested and she began to wear her first pair of glasses, that she discovered all along everyone else had been able to see everything as they travelled home. What else had she been missing and how did this affect her behaviour in a classroom?)

Looking to a solution: Alert his parents and advise them to have his eyes tested and get professional support.

In coming to a new understanding or a different perspective of this person, we are able to find a more lateral and appropriate solution without unnecessary punishment or blame.

B: Unravelling Situations

The 'Why? Why? Why?' chains can be applied to getting to the root cause of a situation. The following is an example, modelling how you can apply this same procedure to all manner of situations. Again, it is when the light-bulb moment illuminates the room, that you come to understand the usefulness of this technique.

Read the following to your students/teenagers. Explain: 'This story comes from an experience of the author, Margaret Hepworth. Listen carefully because halfway through the story I am going to pause and ask you, 'What would you do?"

> Recently, I ran a workshop for primary school students who came from a very poor socio-economic background. For privacy, I won't name the country in which this story takes place. The messages in the workshop were all about conflict resolution and anger management. We watched video-clips, shared stories and ideas, and even performed a role-play that teaches children to use words, not fists, to sort out a problem—from being aggressive to being assertive. These young students appeared to have understood the crux of the lessons and really enjoyed the input. I said a hearty goodbye to them, leaving them in a happy state of self-discovery.
>
> As they filed out of the room, I heard a loud 'whack!' I turned to discover their teacher had used a ruler to hit one child hard enough to create a sharp sound and a yelp from the child. I was astounded. I let the children leave the room and invited the teacher to stay. We sat down together.

Pause here in the story. Ask your students: 'If you were the facilitator of this workshop on anger management and this had just happened, what would you do now?' Discuss, inviting many different opinions. Then continue reading:

> Thoughts raced through my head and I struggled to speak in a calm voice. What part of the concepts in this workshop had this teacher not understood? Surely the link between the teacher whacking a child, and that child then whacking another, was painfully obvious. Yet, as we spoke, I realized it wasn't obvious to her. She agreed that children shouldn't hit each other and that she had previously witnessed what often began as 'hitting out' or pushing and shoving, rapidly turning into a nasty fight. Yet she believed it was necessary for her to use her ruler as corporal punishment to control her class. We talked at length and I, more calmly now, began to employ Einstein's Theory of Why? Why? Why? I was seeking to understand the root cause of the situation.

In small groups of four or five, examine this question: What was the root cause for this teacher to think it was okay to hit a child? Keep moving through the Why? Why? Why? chain to get as deep an answer as you can. Each time someone offers an answer, ask 'And why do you think that is?' Share your ideas with the whole class, realizing that your ideas are 'guesses' at what the root cause is because this teacher is not here to speak with you. However, your 'guesses' are also highly likely to be exactly right! Go back to where we paused halfway through the story and look at your answers to 'What would you do?'

Now, imagining that your 'root cause' is correct, 'What might you do now?' Take a minute of intentional silence before you invite responses. Is your answer the same or different? Do the two responses have a different feel about them? Is one more reactive and the other more responsive?

Teacher's note: To understand intentional silence, refer to Chapter Five, The Conundrum of Inner Listening.

Share this with the class: 'In examples such as this, there is no doubt that we need to address the *immediate situation*. Yet when we stop to find the root cause, we may also find *long-term solutions*. What is the difference between the two? An extension of this is when someone is being bullied at school, we need to address the immediate situation. Yet we also need to get to the root cause. Why should we help the bully as well as the person being bullied? Ah, another why! If we don't get to the root cause, we may allay the situation at hand but we will not alter things in the long run. We can help the "bully" by helping to alleviate their own suffering. They *can* become a decent and respectful adult. We are thereby helping build a better future community.'

Teacher's and parents' note: A second situation, involving domestic violence, has been posted on my website www.thegandhiexperiment.com. The question is posed: What is the root cause of domestic violence? I recently had a profound experience in a workshop for women. A small group of us had begun a session specifically examining how to put peace into practice. To make the work meaningful and relevant, the topic raised was domestic violence. We were asking the question, 'What would you do if you realized someone you knew was a victim of domestic violence.' What emerged, as we applied the 'Why? Why? Why?' chains, moved well beyond our expectations of where this conversation might travel. Read about it on my website.

C. Unravelling the Big Questions in Our World

Here we take any issues or questions that our students might raise, in relation to what is going on 'out there' in our world. The following is a guidance activity to model this.

What is The Root Cause of War? (This is an excellent group activity.)

Ask your students to sit in small groups of four. Present them with this question: 'What is the root cause of war?' For each 'cause of war' that someone in the group presents, the others in the group ask 'And why is that?' Keep asking why and see where the answer travels to. When they complete one 'chain', they can offer a new one.

For example, some common responses have included:

- Poverty can cause war.
- Religion is the cause of many wars.
- Greed has caused war.

'Why? Why is this so?' Keep asking why. Don't stop this 'chain' till you reach a deeper understanding, a light-bulb moment. Allow time for three or four 'chains' to unravel to a much deeper root cause than the seemingly obvious. Draw the group back together and share their responses. Look for common threads between groups. Stop the conversation for a minute. Hold complete silence. Allow people to think over what has been said. Look for wisdom and insights. Have 'new thoughts' come to the group? Has there been a light-bulb, aha moment about war?

Even when the root causes come all the way down to

greed, ego, over-competitiveness, control, manipulation, keep asking 'why?' 'Why do you think *that* person sought control? Where do you think *that* behaviour stems from?' When you go as deeply as you can, pause to look at the root causes laid out before you.

Then, back in small groups, ask: What are the long-term solutions to no more wars occurring on earth?

You may be met by this type of response: 'That is impossible. War will always be part of our lives.' Say this: 'If you did know the answer, what are the long-term solutions to no more wars occurring on this earth?' This will allow for conscious blockages to be released and for the students to move more deeply into the question. Note the emphasis on long-term solutions and on addressing the root causes only.

Teacher's and parents' note: Take your students through The Utopian Scale, Chapter Three, to allow them to understand the full benefits of optimism through 'hope in action'.

The following notes provide an example guide for you to read and refer to during the full group discussion. Further example guides can be found in video clips at www.thegandhiexperiment.com

Example 1: 'Religion has been the cause of many wars.'

'Why is that, do you think?'

'People argue over religion. It creates divisiveness.'

'Not all people argue over religion. There are people practising different religions side by side all over the globe and yet there is no conflict. So return to why or what is the root cause of a religious war.'

'Certain people create intense divisiveness. They use

religion to stir up others, to create a war.'

'So, essentially, people create war? Why would those people create a war?'

And continue—Why? Why? Why?

Example 2: 'Poverty is a cause of war.'

'Why does poverty cause war?'

'Poverty creates situations of extreme inequality. It means people might do things they wouldn't normally do.'

'Yet there are millions of people in poverty who are not engaged in war, or in physical conflict of any kind. Let's return to 'why?' Why might a war or armed conflict begin in a poverty-stricken area?'

And continue asking Why? Why? Why?

Example 3: Perhaps we need to start a new chain: Why is there poverty?

And continue asking Why? Why? Why?

Allow your students to understand that this type of learning, digging deeply into the root causes of the big issues on our planet, could be a game changer for the planet and therefore their own futures.

D. Unravelling Yourself

Now we dig even deeper. Einstein's Theory of Why? Why? Why? can be used on yourself! You need to be brave enough to pursue this 'Why? Why? Why?' chain. Sit quietly and think of a situation you are currently in. It may be that you are arguing with someone close to you.

Example: 'Why am I so angry with my sister that I have stopped talking to her?'

Response: 'She did *'this'* to me!'
The why's can lead down a number of trails:

- Why do I think she did that?
- Why am I continuing to not speak with her?

Keep going calmly, without emotion, follow the 'why' trails. The answers are sometimes astounding, even for ourselves and our own behaviour.

'Why am I behaving like this? Because I am unhappy?' Light-bulb moment. Think about that! Then, be an Einstein and don't stop there. 'Why am I unhappy?' Sometimes there is a realization, 'My unhappiness has nothing whatsoever to do with my sister. It's just that she's the easiest person to take it out on.'

Do you know why? 'Because she is my sister, and deep down inside I believe she will forgive me and return to me.'

E. Unravelling 'Change Begins with Me'

Now we are going to combine the 'Why? Why? Why?' method with the Gandhian principle that 'Change begins with me.'

Examples we could apply are numerous, you will easily find examples that apply directly to you simply by having a few minutes of intentional silence. This particular example is for you adults. Yes, change also begins with you!

Question: 'Why do I hit my child/my students as a form of discipline?'

Response: 'Because sometimes they are out of control and they need discipline.'

Question: 'But why are they "out of control"? Why do I choose hitting as the punishment?'

Continue—'Why? Why? Why?'

Light-bulb moment—'Ah, I was hit as a child by my parents/by my teacher/by my friends. I came to believe that hitting was a way of stopping misbehaviour, or of regaining control.'

Now: 'Change begins with me.' Say it loud and clear—'*Change begins with me.*' Is there a better alternative to disciplining a child than hitting them? What does hitting them actually teach them? If it is supposed to teach them to behave, then why do they keep misbehaving?

When do I hit them? When *I* am tired; when *I* am stressed; when *I* am out of control; when *I* just don't know what else to do? Change begins with me. 'Is there another way?'

Oh absolutely there is. We can use this same framework, combining the 'Why? Why? Why?' chains with 'Change begins with me' to any of our behaviour or choices we are making in our lives that we know deep inside *just doesn't feel right*. We know there is another way, yet we are unsure of how to change.

If we want to create a happier world, then begin with a happier relationship with your children, your partner and with yourself. Choose a violence-free childhood for your children. And by *your* children, I mean *all our* children.

Once we understand the why, then we will open to the appropriate steps to take next, in a calm and measured way that will produce more positive results.

Teacher's and parents' note: Violence begets violence. As parents and educators, we all know the importance of being a role model. There are ways of disciplining children that will help guide them to make more mature decisions and choices. No matter how much we preach non-violence, if we hit children, we are teaching violence. The point is we don't know which child will go on to become the next principal of a school, CEO of a business or leader of our country, or more close to home, parents. Surely we want all our children to grow up with the ability to model a calmer way to resolve conflict. No violence in childhood will certainly equate to less violence in adulthood. If you are in a school where nobody hits the students, don't just sit back and smugly say, 'Well we don't do that.' Become an advocate and help teach others not to do it too. This is a game-changer for the world.

Einstein's Theory of Why? Why? Why? is a solution-focused activity. Often when we encounter difficulty, we shift into the moaning, complaining phase, and we want to stay stuck there because it is easier to do so. And hey, our pride has been hurt so we want to sit with our sorrows for a while, often for a long while. Take this note from Gandhi, 'Suffering has its limits.' By taking three deep breaths and engaging in the 'Why? Why? Why?' we will shift ourselves beyond our own ego and engage in something much more important, finding a solution. Video clips are available at www.thegandhiexperiment.com modelling example guides of using Einstein's Theory of Why? Why? Why?

Five

The Conundrum of Inner Listening

*Why are we all seeking wisdom without,
when there is so much wisdom within?*

GANDHI called it the still, small voice; Eckhart Tolle, writes of an inner essence, a planetary consciousness that we become aware of when contemplating the ethereal flower, crystal or bird (A New Earth, 2005 Eckhart Tolle, Penguin); the Buddha spoke of an awakening to a deep awareness within. It's been variously called connecting with the Collective Consciousness; meeting your higher self; opening to your intuition; awakening to yourself; becoming conscious and more. Some believe we are speaking with the Divine within. The Prophet Mohammed (SAWS) asked, 'Is it not true these are words from your Deepest Being?' Charlie Chaplin, inspirational actor/director of the 1940s, said it is, 'not in one man, nor a group of men; but in all men (women), in You!' This is the finding of your inner voice. Some people pray, some meditate, some reflect. Some chant or sing. Whilst others sit quietly and listen. Just listen.

Whatever form it takes, learning to use intentional silence, or 'own time', and what comes through the silence, is an important tool in guidance of self. We constantly teach our children to 'look out'. How much time do we give in the school curriculum to 'looking in'? The earlier in life we learn to use this, the better. Gandhi came to rely upon his still, small voice, his inner voice, as a guidance he trusted to follow. A voice that provided solutions when his way was barred; a voice that gave hope; a voice that kept him on his path to achieve his goals, with integrity. Often we are listening to the calls of materialism over our own inner voice of guidance. Through our inner voice we can learn patience, courage and integrity.

My son, James Tyler, has recently begun his own practice of mindful guidance. He takes a holistic approach to life education. He tells me, 'The inner voice can be found anytime and anywhere. Some people find it through music, art, sport, meditation or being in nature. What all of these share is the tendency to bring you into the here and now. Your inner voice exists only in the present moment; that is where it will be heard, where there are no "thoughts" as such; just you and the moment of "no mind".'

Interestingly, more and more religious and non-religious people are instituting a connection with their inner voice as a daily practice. Individuals taking ten minutes of quiet time in the morning; people coming together in small groups to hold intentional silence, then to share insights afterwards. There are even those pausing mid staff meeting for a minute's silence, for colleagues and peers to settle the busyness of a meeting and to allow consolidation, clarity of thought, new insights to emerge, not overrun by emotion. It is a practice bearing much fruit in terms of collective understanding.

Having had extraordinary experiences at the temple at Shirdi, India, I recently asked myself, what would Sai Baba of Shirdi have called this inner voice? It came to me that he might call it 'The Gift'. People often honour others with a compliment: 'You have a gift!' Mozart had a gift for music, Salvador Dali, a gift for art. Our talent is perhaps our gift, and talents come in many forms. At the conclusion of one of my workshops, an Indian IT technician once said to me 'Your energy is a gift from God.' I remember being surprised and delighted that someone would frame such a thing in this way. Perhaps it is our gift that connects us most deeply with our spirit. It is why when we revel in our talent, we lose time, we feel enlivened and our spirit soars. It is through our spirit that we can find the path to our inner voice.

Gandhi and many of his compatriots, believed that the purpose of Nai Talim, New education or Education for Life, was to effect the realization of the presence of the divine within your soul. Ah, I would love to approach the Minister for Education in Australia and postulate this in amongst the drive for 'academic excellence'! One day I will.

A STORY

One evening I sat very still in a Sufi music group meditation. As the music swirled and danced around me, I went deeper and deeper into myself. Down in the darkness, I threw out an age old question. It is the question of a seeker:

'Can you please give me a sign?'

What came was laughter. Hearty laughter. It paused: 'I'm always giving you signs and you ignore those. Why would I give you one now?' I smiled broadly. I took that as a sign.

LESSON PLAN

Ask your students, 'What does it mean when people talk about an "inner voice"—a voice of inner guidance?' There is no one 'correct answer'. Allow them to unpack the question in any way they choose. Then read them the introductory passages above, from this chapter.

Share this: 'There are several "conundrums" when it comes to the art of inner listening. Several "puzzles" that can appear to block our way to reaching our inner selves. Sometimes it is as though we are in a labyrinth, twisting and turning, this way and that. Until one day, through steady practice, we seem to have a direct path. Indeed some days it's like a four lane freeway, straight to our destination.'

Share the following lessons with your students/children. Take your time with each activity. Finding your inner voice takes time and practice. There is a beautiful saying: 'Find yourself ten quiet minutes to listen to your inner guidance every day. And if you are too busy and don't have the time, then make sure you give yourself an hour.'

The First Conundrum: Is this My Inner Voice?

Share the following with your class, for discussion.

For most of us, the minute we sit still, a nagging voice appears:

- You haven't done this.

- Why are you sitting still? You haven't finished your tasks!
- Are you seriously asking for that? You are not deserving enough!
- You are not good enough!

And on and on it goes. Is this the voice of inner listening that we are trying to open up to? In a word, no. The conundrum is this—there *appear* to be *two* inner voices, one is always telling you off, even degrading you. This is the voice of the inner critic. And rarely does the inner critic do you any good! If someone else spoke to you in this manner, you would be very hurt. You would either 'fight back' or retreat into yourself further, perhaps both. So why would you want to do this to yourself? So, instead of demanding of yourself, 'Agh, why haven't you done this?' ask, 'What good things have I done today?' List your achievements, even small ones. Or calmly say to yourself, 'Thanks for reminding me of that. I'll get to that later.'

The inner voice we are seeking is a calm voice of guidance. This voice builds self-esteem, lets you know you *are* good enough. This inner voice is always open, settled, exploratory and constructive. It may be challenging, yet it aims to have a positive outcome. And you know it. Your inner voice will take you on a journey where doors open for you because you are now in harmony with who you want to be; with who you really are. There is something about this inner voice that resonates, so that, by your senses, you know this to be true.

Inner voice time is about sitting still, or walking quietly, digging deep, and accessing, being open to your inner voice of guidance. And releasing yourself from ego. This is not a time of asking for something, 'Dear God, I would like a pony.' You may want to begin with some thoughts of gratitude. However, what you are really doing is simply opening yourself up to listening, deep listening.

Questions

- Have you ever heard the voice of your inner critic? What does it sound like to you? What effect does it have on you?
- Do you think you have ever experienced the voice of inner guidance? Do you recall what the guidance or thoughts were? How did this feel for you?

There are many pathways to find your inner voice. Here are several to try.

Cheryl Wood of Initiatives of Change, Australia, has made a practice of finding time for inner listening, for decades. She now teaches this practice in life purpose workshops. When I asked her to describe how we can find our inner voice, this is what she wrote for me. Read it through, then follow it as a practice.

'Inner Listening is the most valuable tool you can ever learn if you want to live a fulfilled and adventurous life. Sitting quietly, being in nature, in your favourite quiet place, emptying your mind of stresses and pressures, you might be surprised what comes forward in your mind. It is also a good practice to write down a thought as it comes and you can be ready for any others. This also gives a chance to later look at what came and consider what action you might be meant to take, if any, following your listening time.'

Take your students outside. Find plenty of grassy space for them to sit quietly, on their own. For larger groups, it may be best to set this one as 'homework' so they can really find their own space and not be disturbed. Print off the following passages (i) to (iv) and give to each student to read when they are quiet and on their own. It would be good for them to take a pen and paper to write their thoughts down.

(i) Sitting or lying on the grass, stare into it for a long time. Staring into it, eventually you will begin to notice things you've never noticed before; you will see movement you have never seen, and experience life up close, appearing closer and more vibrant, somehow more 'real'. Something wonderful or intriguing will happen, down there in the world of the grass. When it does, enjoy it for what it is. Then open yourself to your higher self. When you find yourself in this space, new realizations will come to you about yourself, about the world, about the universe.

(ii) Read this list of 'Realizations' that may come, simply by staring into a grassy patch and observing:

- there are so many protective devices within nature, it seems natural to seek protection.
- the depth of beauty, awe and wonder that can come from something as simple as staring into a flower.

Reflect on this.

- we think the grass is still and yet it seems to be constantly moving
- so much decay and so much life, mingled together,

one beside the other. The decay feeds new life
- complexity and simplicity in one tiny patch
- nature is teeming with relationships of all kinds
- who decides who or what is a weed?
- sunlight gives you serotonin. Serotonin gives you hope; makes you feel good. Wow, the sunlight literally gives you hope! But too much sunlight might give you cancer! What is this telling me about moderation? Part of the beauty of being out here in the sun, on the grass is I have given myself time away from busyness. It feels very good.

Add your own realizations to the list as they come to you. They can be anything at all, no restrictions. Then look at your list. What do you think your inner voice is telling you by reaching out and connecting with nature?

(iii) Ask a butterfly about its past life as a caterpillar. Does it recall ever being a caterpillar? How could it possibly believe it ever was? When it was cocooned, was this a form of death? What is death? How did the butterfly emerge so completely transformed? Can I emerge completely transformed?

(iv) Stare again into the grass and ask yourself, 'What do I believe?'

Let's try finding our inner voice by reading a poem. This is Gandhi's Prayer for Peace. You can do this same exercise by reading any poem, or listening to a song and hearing the words, the sound and the vibration.

Tell your students you are going to read them a poem and then they will be asked to sit quietly for one minute. You should have the poem printed out so everyone can see it as well as hear it. Begin:

'Sit quietly for one minute with the thoughts of the poem. Be aware of what comes to mind. Your thoughts may be directly related to the words of the poem or may take you somewhere else. Be very aware of where, or to whom, these thoughts take you.'

Gandhi's Prayer for Peace

I offer you peace.
I offer you love.
I offer you friendship.
I see your beauty.
I hear your need.
I feel your feelings.
My wisdom flows from the highest source.
I salute that source in you.
Let us work together.
For unity and peace.

(i) The scene in this poem is as though two people are sitting face to face, looking directly into each other's eyes. Read the poem again, perhaps several times. Each time you read it, imagine two people who may be currently seen as oppositional, saying this poem to each other. For example, an Israeli and a Palestinian, a white supremacist with a Chinese-American, one world leader to another, a logger with a 'greenie'. Imagine what may have happened if the British had

said this to the Native Americans, or the French to the Vietnamese, the Romans to the Jews of Bethlehem.
(ii) Braver still, can you say the poem to someone you know? If not, then perhaps just turn to the person next to you, place your hands together and say, 'Namaste.' It means 'I see you in me.' Be mindful of your thoughts; be aware of the way your body responds; be conscious of your feelings.

My friend Bernadette will often begin a guided meditation like this: 'Stare directly at the candle. Stare into the flame. Breathe deeply and hold each breath for three seconds. On the third breath shut your eyes and take the light of the candle into you...'

Another friend, David, will begin a mediation with: 'It is your time now...'

Dr Ghanshyam Sharma is a prestigious yoga teacher in Mumbai. In his class, each time you make the next yoga movement, he will say, 'Now feel the change.' He will focus us in on our breath and say, 'Breathing can never be of the past or the future; breathing can only be of the present.'

Sit quietly and try one or all of these 'introductions' to still yourself. It is all about being present to the moment. Once present, pause, listen. Be aware of the thoughts, images and sensations that will come. When they come, let them sit, then write them down.

If you are religious, sit and connect deeply with the tenets of your religion. If you are not religious, yet you are spiritual, connect deeply with your spirituality. If you believe you are neither religious nor spiritual, connect deeply with the best humanity can be.

Inner Listening

Quotes

These are examples from friends whom I have been with during times of inner listening.

Sue, she had a whole raft of them, they were just flowing. The good thing was she wrote them down so she could reflect on them, and so we get to share them.

Don't be a follower: create paths of thought that are your own.

Seek not what you think you need but allow what comes to you. Open your heart to hope.

As humans, we are not here to attain perfection...we are here to be human!

This one in particular meant a lot to me—*Sleep softly upon the earth as the sky opens up your soul.*

Chintan shared: *Self-nourishment is an investment too.*

Bernadette: *Peace is your heritage; peace and harmony are your right.*

Another friend: *He doesn't make me feel worthless—just less.*

For me, many quotes have come. Here are three:

People say, 'I want to be the best person I can be,' or 'I want to be the healthiest person I can be.' What would happen if you asked yourself to be the best spirit or soul you could possibly be?

This is where you are today; and today you build from here.

And from my meditation in the Golden Temple in Amritsar:

When the sword becomes words, then it will be done.

These are Gandhi's:

*An eye for eye only ends up making the whole world blind.
Happiness is when what you think, what you say, and what you do are in harmony.*

From a guru—*The old energy is asking for a new response.*

Many songs and poems are written through the inner voice. Songwriters are often overheard to say, 'It is as though it came from nowhere.' I imagine these lines appeared this way.

*Love dares you to change our way of
caring about ourselves*
Under Pressure: David Bowie, Freddie Mercury

Read this passage to your students and discuss.

> Sometimes we are so overwhelmed by hurt and pain, that we can think that the only way out of 'my problem' is to hurt or maim, to seek revenge, to humiliate, perhaps even to kill. If this happens, then you are nowhere near your inner voice of guidance. You are sitting with ego, with lower energies, which exist within us all. Recognize this for what it is, a reaction to the pain. We have evolved physically. It's time to evolve socially and emotionally. Go back to being still, listen again and again and again. If need be, walk, run, throw yourself into physical sport. Or cry. Have a really good, cathartic cry. Then return to listen to your higher self, the collective consciousness, God, the Universe. And find that path that is guided by love and seeks no harm, for yourself and for others.

The Second Conundrum: The Expansive Universe Within

Ask your class 'Where is the universe? Point to it.' It is highly likely that most of them will point outside. Up to the sky and beyond. Ask them to describe the universe: What does it look like? Where exactly is it? Some of them will point within.

Explain to them, there is a whole universe within each one of us. Ask them to shut their eyes, focus on their breathing. When you *focus in, in, in,* an *expansive universe opens up before you,* a place of never-ending possibility. Try this now.

Another 'way in' is to contemplate this: In fact, your body itself is a universe, filled with millions of atoms, every atom containing microscopic parts. There are things going on in our bodies that we are consciously unaware of, trillions of 'parts' that function to create the 'whole'. If we focus on this miracle alone, with our eyes closed, going deeper and deeper into ourselves, we find an expansive, never ending place where we can meet our unconscious selves, our higher selves. Some call this God. You may call it anything you like!

Take your students on a guided meditation. The more practised they become at this, the more they can tune inwards, their unconscious minds will allow them to connect with their inner voice. There are guided meditations offered on www.thegandhiexperiment.com Once you are used to these, you will be able to create your own.

Story of the Secluded 'Holy Person'

Read the story aloud.

> A Holy Person chose to reside alone for three years, in a deep secluded forest. No other human saw the Holy

Person and the Holy Person saw no other human. The forest provided all that was required to satiate the Holy Person's physical needs. Some time was spent wandering, eating, creating a shelter. Most of the time was spent in a deep internal journey. All of the time was spent in mindful presence. Every moment was spent in the awakened now.

Finally, after three years, a span of time both measured as long and brief, the Holy Person emerged from the forest and was reunited with others. She brought with her powerful messages for love and peace on earth. A message of enlightenment, that all who heard it immediately understood. She could now speak for hours, a wise sage. Groups would gather to hear her and seek her counsel. She would always finish her gatherings with this wisdom. 'We are all divine energy and all I have to do is help you remember that.'

Questions

- Why do you think the Holy Person went into the forest in the first place? Why did there seem to be a need for isolation?
- What is your interpretation of the Holy Person's message—'We are all divine energy and all I have to do is help you remember that.'
- This woman had entered the forest, seeking wisdom—being open to new learning. She carried no books, no pens, no mobile phone, no internet. She spoke to no other human in three years. So where did this new-found wisdom come from?

The Third Conundrum: You Don't Always Immediately Understand the Message!

Remarkably, solutions will often come through inner guidance in the form of a name, 'Go and talk to so and so'. Or a suggestion, 'Perhaps try saying this...' Or an idea, like a light-bulb moment, 'I've never thought of that before!' But sometimes what you hear is like a mystical puzzle, or a wisp of a tangled poem. At times the message feels steeped in profound wisdom; it can be like watching one of those movies where an ancient guru hands a young person a message and they must traverse their personal journey to unravel it. I must admit, I love it when that happens!

When this comes, don't over think the message. Allow it to sit. Invariably over the next few days or weeks you will come to know what it means.

Here are a few that have come to me:

Solve the jigsaw; the wisdom lies ready within you
Don't meditate under the tree; meditate with the tree
We need the sound of children's laughter across the world
Christ's wounds have healed
Everything has a reason; now go out and meet your reason
Accept the proffered hand

A Personal Story of Inner Voice; Inner Direction

Through sharing my inner voice, I hope you will get to know me better. I hope you find someone, or many someones, to share your inner voice with too. Here is a story of a day I heard my inner voice with remarkable clarity. One morning, in that liminal moment between sleeping and waking, I heard a very clear voice: 'Go to India where it all began'. I think the fact that I was used to meditating was what allowed me to hear it. A pathway had been opened. I remember jumping out of bed and asking, 'Where what began? Gandhi? Buddha? Hinduism? What are we talking about here?'

What did I do with this message? At first I ignored it. I didn't have time to go to India! That would come eventually when I could afford the time and finances for a holiday, maybe in a few years.

But the message persisted in different ways. A friend invited me to come to India to meditate with her. I couldn't go, bad timing. A bank manager asked me to talk over writing her deceased husband's memoirs, he had been an Indian civil servant. This meeting twigged my memory 'Go to India' but still I refrained from really listening. Over the next few months, time and time again India was staring me in the face. When finally I met the National Coordinator of Initiatives of Change, Australia, in that very first meeting, she said to me, 'We have a conference in India, I think you should go.' I gave in. I wanted to reply, 'I know I should go, I just don't know why.' Following that message from my inner voice, 'Go to India where it all began,' has become a major turning point in my life, connecting me in with educators and others across India, with further guidance and inspirational ideas coming to life, even eventually taking me into Pakistan. I have since, more and more, learned to act upon this 'still, small voice' of guidance. To open to my intuition, my connectedness, with that who I really am; conscious energy.

I went to India, and it all began. The Gandhi Experiment:

world peace through education.

Where could your still, small voice take you?

A Friend's Story

To my friend, Sue Stewart, who belongs to the meditation group I regularly attend (run by another friend Bernadette Hugh-Clink), her inner voice flows through poetry. I have witnessed Sue, in mid conversation, find that flow. I have seen her pick up a pen and within ten minutes a poem finds itself birthed on her page. I have observed friends sit back—'Wow, where did that come from?' Sue usually replies, 'I don't know. It just comes.' So I have asked her again, in a quiet moment, to share with us where she thinks this poetry is emanating from:

> While contemplating how my inner voice actually worked, I instantly began to over think the whole thing. My mind took me to a whole range of flowery analogies, for example: it's like pulling back a heavy curtain to let the sunlight flow over and through me. This was actually fluff and nonsense that just sounded pretty. Really it is far simpler and far less poetic—I take a thought or a subject and place it in my mind to simply contemplate it. I allow it to just be there, without trying to "make" something of it. I allow it to open in its own way. I do not judge its path or try to change it, I allow it to run free and watch as it grows in my mind. As the thought/subject/idea starts to grow, the words begin to form and I feel compelled to put pen to paper and transfer this inner voice to a palpable outer voice. Sometimes the need to transfer the inner voice is soooo strong that no matter

what I am doing, I *must stop*, and write. I have been driving my car and have had to find the closest parking spot and pull over so I could jot down a poem or note that has been pounding in my head to be let out. That inner voice must be allowed its freedom/transformation, otherwise it is lost.

Here is one of Sue's beautiful poems. What I find interesting is that the poem's message is as much for all of us as it is for Sue.

New World

To see this world
With brand new eyes
To experience life
Knowing no previous lies
To tread this rich earth
With uncalloused feet
To splash in life's pond
Each experience replete
To know the sun's kiss
On an innocent cheek
To gaze at the moon
With no answers to seek
To view nature's gifts
With an unbounded awe
To rush at each moment
Just wishing for more
To learn life's hard lesson
With a heart open wide
To believe with clear truth

> *That time's on your side*
> *To live this fresh life*
> *With a soul bright and new*
> *To fill every day*
> *There is so much to do.*

'Moonlight Meanderings' by Sue Stewart

RESOURCES

There are many resources for meditating, finding quiet time, exploring your inner voice. It is a journey most definitely worth taking and one I believe will help us unravel many of life's 'unsolvable' problems. We just need to be open to stepping on the pathway. A few guided meditations can be found at www.thegandhiexperiment.com. Another of Sue Stewart's poems, 'No More Crucifixion', a compelling piece, can be found in one of The Gandhi Experiment's resources for teachers and parents: Lessons on line www.thegandhiexperiment.com The Fourth Conundrum of Inner Listening is revealed in the sequel to this book: *The Gandhi Experiment: Teaching our Teenagers Mindful Activism.*

Six

The 'Call It What It Is' Theory of Life

This one is really simple, as simple as it gets. So often we judge or are judged by others. We make assumptions about things, events and people, without exploring the reality of our speculations. This lesson, 'The Call It What It Is' theory of life, works on the simple action of naming something for what it is. This aids us in removing the negative responses that can arise—the power play, the sense of control, the exclusion—when somebody successfully parades as being superior to somebody else.

Let's begin with some discursive thoughts:

- Is it possible to feel humble and proud all at the same time? Isn't that a contradiction?
- How can you feel proud of an achievement, yet not superior or arrogant?
- How do our beliefs about ourselves and others impact our behaviour?
- Why do we so often judge people?

How did Gandhi manage to remain humble when hundreds of millions of people turned, with their faces lifted upwards, towards him? People lined up daily seeking Gandhi's advice; *his* answers to *their* problems. How did he not feel a sense of superiority over them, that he 'had something', some mysterious power, that they did not? How do you think he stayed humble? Let's get real when people acquire fame, whether it is wanted or unwanted, what tends to follow is a huge swelling of their own egoist sense of importance to all around them.

I'm not sure of the answers. I wonder if it was an inner demon he had to fight? How would things have been different if he had decided he was infinitely superior to everyone around him scrambling for his attention? I guess the answers lie somewhere in Gandhi choosing simplicity as a way of life; in his ability to remain fragile and vulnerable; to hold grace; and definitely in humour—the laughter shared with the staunchest of political allies to the little child who came to visit and sit beside him. Shared laughter is a wonderful leveller.

How do we learn not to judge others? How do we learn to not accept another's judgement of us? To remain 'levelled'? We become confused by other people's attitudes towards us.

At these times, we may discover a clarity brought about by simply naming things; to call these things what they are—racism, homophobia, sexism, gender inequality, jealousy, arrogance, etc. In doing so, we take the first step to diffuse our emotional reactions, to help us take control of our own responses, and in many cases, to help the person aiming these attacks, understand exactly what it is they are doing. Sometimes this will help them to alter their behaviour, sometimes not. Let us remember, in the end, we can only own our own behaviour, not the behaviour of others.

Here is a story of Gandhi owning his own behaviour.

People would line up for hours, patiently or otherwise, awaiting their turn to see Gandhiji. Their need? To ask him the questions they had been puzzling over and could not find a satisfactory answer for themselves. Some just wanted to meet him, see him, touch him, touch his feet in quiet respect. Others had very specific requests.

One day, a woman joined the line, standing in the heat with her young son. The boy did not wish to be there. But dutifully, or otherwise, held his mother's hand and watched as the line inched closer to this enigma of a man. This man was indeed, his hero, and his mother knew it. Finally, it was mother and son's turn to step forward and come face to face with this small framed, bespectacled man dressed only in a swaddled white cloth, Gandhiji. The boy listened as his mother put forth her plea, 'Bapu, my son is addicted to sugar. Please Bapu, it is having a very negative effect on him–his health, his behaviour. We have tried and tried to make him stop. But nothing will do this. He respects you. Please tell him to stop eating the sugar.'

The boy looked up, expecting a recriminating smack of angry words across his cheeks. But Bapu spoke quietly. 'Please come back in two weeks.' The boy didn't know whether to be relieved or worried. 'No unkind words, no telling me I can't eat sugar. But we have to line up again? Really?' he thought to himself.

Two weeks went by and the boy found himself back in the line. This time it felt longer and hotter. Surely they could go straight to the front of the line; after all they had been there once before and Gandhji himself had asked them to return.

But instead they waited. And inched. And inched. Forward.

Finally, they reached the front of the line. There he was again, Bapu, looking ever the same. Patient. Kind-eyed. His mother stepped forward, more determined this time to get the answer she was seeking. 'Please Bapu, my son is addicted to sugar. Please make him stop!'

Gandhi, turned to the boy, reached his hand gently to his cheek. 'Ah, I have been waiting.' The boy would have been scared, but the hand on his cheek was soft and assuring. 'Please stop eating sugar. For your own health and for the sake of your parents, in respect for them, you must give up eating sugar.'

The mother was grateful and yet somewhat shocked. 'I must ask you, if that is all it takes, why did we need to return two weeks from our first request? Why could you not have told him that then and saved us our time and effort?'

Gandhi smiled. 'Two weeks is how long it has taken me to give up eating sugar,' he said.

No judgement, no labelling, no recrimination, no sense of superiority. Instead a recognition: 'I cannot look at another person and make a judgement, if I cannot look at myself first.'

At an earlier time, Gandhi had invited a family of 'untouchables' to join him and his compatriots at their Sabarmati Ashram, in Ahmedabad. For those living in the ashram, this caused a mixed reaction; joy for some, great pain for others. Having been raised within the Hindu caste system, the 'untouchables', literally were deemed, and doomed, untouchable. Gandhi renamed them the Harijans, God's people. Certain members of the ashram threatened to leave should they be forced to mix with people of a caste regarded as 'so low', these people had no caste. This was the point that Gandhi 'called it what it is': Discrimination. Those casting judgement were asked to leave the ashram; the Harijans remained.

Through this experience, many people learnt lessons of great humility; others refused to learn anything at all. Through the years, many have spoken for the untouchables, now called Dalits. It was a Dalit, Dr Ambedkar, who authored the Indian Constitution. Today, issues of discrimination against the Dalits still remain. If we can 'call it what it is', we will learn to no longer judge the 'book' by its 'cover'. Let's apply the 'Call It What It Is' theory to ourselves as parents and teachers. One way in which it will most certainly help is if we stop making judgements about the courses our children enter beyond their secondary schooling. When we can 'call it what it is'—a Medical degree is for those who have an interest and aptitude in the area of medicine. A Law Degree, a Bachelor of Music, a Certificate in Massage Therapy, a Bachelor of Arts, a Building Degree, a Certificate in Hospitality—all follow suit. Hands on trades are as vital and necessary as any of other career. Let's not create elitism around jobs. Instead let's acknowledge the validity and dignity of each and every occupation.

You may have heard this well known quote, perhaps misattributed to Einstein: 'Everybody is a genius. But if you judge a fish by its ability to climb a tree, it will live its whole life believing that it is stupid.' It sums up the situation succinctly.

If every day you call a child stupid, I will give you one guess as to how that child will begin acting. Yes, 'stupid'! And the day that 'stupid' child does something remarkable and outstanding in the field of, let's say, art, is the day you will need to eat your words! The day you walk into the music room to discover the girl who, in your history class, cannot write a research essay to save herself, is now sitting at the piano belting out a tune as though she were Adele herself, is the day the depth of the reality of such a simple tool, the 'Call It What It Is' Theory of Life, will truly humble you.

Let's stop *judging*; let's become *curious* about our children. Allow them to learn about themselves. Allow them to be happy and not judged in their own skin. Allow them to flourish in what it is they love doing. Allow them to simply be. Whilst Einstein's Theory of Why? Why? Why? is very useful for helping us to ascertain the root cause of an issue, the 'Call It What It Is' theory of life, is an excellent tool for naming the problem and removing the emotional judgement surrounding it.

LESSON PLAN

1. The 'Call It What It Is' Theory of Life

Read your students the following passage[8] (Rosie O'Dea in *Clarity in Time*):

> Call it what it is. If someone is physically stronger than you, it does not make them superior. It simply makes them physically stronger. Likewise, if you have more wealth than that person over there, again, it doesn't make you superior. Yes, it does mean you are wealthier. But that is all it means. Say your friend, Rahul is deemed to be academically smarter than you—he's won the Academic Achievement Award at school. That doesn't make him

---

[8]Hepworth, Margaret (2012), *Clarity in Time*. Balboa Press

superior to you. It may not even mean he understands and interprets certain things more quickly than you. Marita may be seen as the most beautiful girl in the school. She's been declared culturally and contextually beautiful. To ram home a point, this doesn't make her superior. Although it may change her behaviour. None of these things make you or anyone else superior. And if anyone thinks for one minute that they are superior, then their thinking is flawed. And they have proven they are not!

Questions

- In one sentence, write what you think this passage is saying. Now, discuss the passage with your whole class.
- Has there ever been a time when you felt 'inferior' to someone else? You don't need to write this down, think back to that time. How would things have been different if you had been able to 'call it what it is'?
- The 'Call It What It Is' theory of life can be a useful tool for us time and time again, as we fall into the same old traps of jealousy, lack of self-worth, and self-doubt. When you're feeling down and doing that negative talk, 'I'm not as good as so and so,' call it what it is. That other person may be a creative artist, a productive worker, a powerful bike rider, a brilliant mathematician, but it doesn't make them superior. Remind yourself of the things you are good at doing, your strengths. Make this self-reflection one of your strengths. However, remember this also: if it is you that

> has a remarkable ability in one area, if for example, it is you who is a champion swimmer, then apply the theory as well—call it what it is. You are a great swimmer. You can be proud of that fact. Yet it doesn't make you superior.

As my friend, Chintan Girish Modi, of Friendships Across Borders Aao Dosti Karein, says: 'Don't be jealous, be joyous!' Be joyous for others' achievements; and don't forget to be joyous of your own.

2. The Story of The Morphing Caterpillar: On Judgement

Read the following story aloud.

> Distracted again, this time in the children's section of this enormous bookshop, I came face to face with a picture book. Oh, I smiled, as if greeting an old friend. The book perched on the display shelf before me, I remembered well. It was the one about the caterpillar who eats so much, he winds up with a big tummy ache. He thinks he has appendicitis but he wakes up as a beautiful butterfly! Too cute. I reached up and pulled the book off the shelf. Time to re-visit my childhood. But the opening line didn't feel familiar at all.
>
> *The ugly caterpillar morphs into a beautiful butterfly.*

Wasn't that the ending? I read on[9].

> *But the caterpillar had never believed he was ugly. That's a human judgement. The caterpillar had always thought*

---

[9]Ibid.

he was nicely plump and fuzzy; cuddly in fact. And a beautiful serene green. When he morphs, it isn't about his beauty. It isn't about wings and freedom. It's just as fun curling your way along a fresh green leaf as it is to flit and float. It's all good! When he morphs, it's simply what happens next. It simply is.

Discuss the passage.

- Who was making the judgement that the caterpillar was ugly and the butterfly was beautiful? Was it the caterpillar or someone else?
- What did the caterpillar feel about being a caterpillar? How did it feel about being a butterfly?
- How can we relate this story to our own lives/our own experiences?
- How does the caterpillar employ the 'Call It What It Is' theory of life?

3. 'Ask About What It Is'—An Extension of 'Call It What It Is.'

Read the following passage to the class:

'Don't judge, be curious.' It's a mantra I have adopted after hearing it at an Initiatives of Change National Gathering. I now teach this phrase to both teachers and students. 'Don't judge, be curious.' It comes in handy as a saviour to all manner of misunderstandings. Your friend has told you something and you cannot for the life of you understand why they would say such a thing. Your partner has commented on something you did, and you are left feeling hurt. I can't begin to tell you how many times I have jumped to conclusions, made assumptions, overreacted to something someone has said or done, only to discover that, when I stop to objectively inquire, 'What did you mean when you said...?' the situation is surprisingly and honestly completely not what I had thought it to be. Often I end up laughing, 'Oh I thought you meant...thank heavens I asked!' Seriously, miscommunication or 'mis-receiving', as I call it, is the cause of far too many entangled arguments.

Questions

- Can you recall a time when you, or someone else, misunderstood something another person was saying or doing? Write a creative writing story about it that explores this miscommunication or 'mis-receiving'.
- Create a short role-play that in Scene One shows a conversation taking place where one person misunderstands and is offended. In Scene Two show what could have happened if the offended person had chosen to ask, 'What did you mean when you said..?' Perform these in your classroom.
- If you have video camera equipment, you could even make a short video-clip about this. I would love to see them!

4. A Third Version of The 'Call It What It Is' Theory— Naming Your Thoughts

I have discovered a very simple yet useful tool that can help unravel jealousy; help keep that ego at bay; and can help you remain focused on a task. Again, this one is so simple and works like a treat! It is 'call it what it is—naming your thoughts'. Read on.

Hold a discussion with your students/teens about the inner workings of their brains; the constant chatter that goes on; your inner critic. (You may like to refer to The Conundrum of Inner Listening to learn more about the inner critic.)

Ask questions such as: Do you compare yourself to other people? Do you put yourself down when you can't seem to do what they can do? Do you find it easier to recognize someone else's talents, but not your own?

The trick is to recognize yourself doing this; to capture that moment. Be mindful as to when your thoughts start this chatter. Then simply repeat these words: 'ego, ego, ego'. For example: I am doing my mathematics homework and my mind begins wandering to my best friend who is a whizz at mathematics. I start thinking, 'Why can't I be like him/her? Why did I get the dumb mathematics brain?' Then off my brain wanders, following this trail of thoughts, creating a picture in my own mind that I will never be good at maths! Stop! Recognize what you are doing. Say 'ego, ego, ego,' and like magic you will be back doing your homework, having removed the dark inner critic.

Remember: our egos don't just tell us how great we are, they also tell us all our flaws. Our ego is our inner critic.

This very same 'trick' works in the case of wandering from the task at hand, e.g. how many of us dive into Facebook when we are supposed to be focusing on another task? Say to yourself: 'distraction, distraction, distraction.' You will find that it is as though a light clicks on in your brain, and you say, 'Oh yeah, I remember what I am supposed to be doing now. I can come back to Facebook later.'

Photo credit: Margaret Hepworth. Gandhi Smriti, Delhi 2014

Sounds too simple? Try it, practise it. It really does work! You are 'calling your thoughts for what they are'! Naming them, 'calling it what it is', calls you into the present moment to be mindful about your thoughts. You are then able to get on with what you are doing and not be drawn down the 'rabbit warren' of negative or distracting thoughts.

In being mindful about your thoughts you are living the mantra, 'Change begins with me.' Sometimes simplicity with purpose is the most effective thing.

Teacher's Note: The Dalits

Gandhi's relationship with the Harijans, or Dalits, and with Dr Ambedkar is hotly debated. It is well worth looking more deeply into this issue, perhaps creating a class project around it, to examine the discrimination against the Dalits which still exists today. It would be useful to also apply the tool, Einstein's Theory of Why? Why? Why? to this issue. Why are there people treated as 'untouchables' in India today?

Seven

Almost Impossible Thoughts

WHAT are 'Almost impossible thoughts'? The phrase itself sounds like a bit of an oxymoron. Yet when you enter the realm of 'Almost impossible thoughts'—anything becomes possible.

It was an 'Almost impossible thought' that Nelson Mandela, having been jailed for twenty-seven years, would ever be released. And nobody would have believed he could go on to become president of South Africa. It was an 'Almost impossible thought' that the Berlin Wall would come tumbling down in 1989, and that Germany, a country divided for so long by war and political tension, would be reunited. For the people of India in the early 1900's, independence from Britain was an 'Almost impossible thought'.

Participants of the 'Almost impossible thoughts' activity are taken on a journey through history and then invited to step forward, now prepared to be the key players in their own design for change by asking: What are your 'Almost impossible thoughts'?

This activity provides hope for change; hope in action. Positive psychologists have shown us the direct link between hope and action. When we become more optimistic about our future, for a number of reasons both physiologically, in the chemicals/hormones released, psychologically and emotionally, we feel a sense of being able to do more, contribute more and move to a point of action. Vice versa also creates the same effect: the more we do, the more we give to others, i.e. the more altruistic we become, we feel a greater sense of optimism. We release despair and despondency. As I outlined in Chapter Three, The Utopian Scale, I have seen this occur with teenagers innumerable times. Teaching mindful activism and role modelling those who have achieved the seemingly impossible, is paving a way forward for young people seeking to make a positive difference.

LESSON PLAN

1. Share and discuss the following passage with your class or children. Print it out to allow them to read it.

Gandhi was a radical thinker. Let that thought sit for a moment. What does it mean? What is it implying? What exactly is a radical thinker? When someone goes against the current status quo, they turn against the tide that is pushing a particular way. This may happen in the political, economic and/or social arenas. Radical thinking or taking radical action can be both positive and negative. That in itself is a choice. Amusingly, this means that if you are the person who stands at a traffic crossing, waiting for the green light to cross, whilst everyone else around you is crossing against a red light, you, in your patience and discipline, are a radical thinker.

Essentially, Mohandas Gandhi had an 'Almost impossible thought'. Simple in essence, enormous in practice, gargantuan in scale. His thought was to use non-violence, non-cooperation and active civil disobedience on a nationwide scale to attain Swaraj, self-rule, from the hands of the British oppressor. Gandhi sought to challenge the British, not the people, but their system. He had an 'Almost impossible thought' that unlike other nations which had attempted, and in some cases achieved, independence through war and armed conflict, Indian self-rule would be achieved by peaceful means. Gandhi was a radical thinker and he stepped into his dream with a non-violent energy, the likes of which had not been witnessed for centuries.

2. Share the following concepts/stories with your students.

You may care to do some further research on each story. However, it is also sufficient to share just this much. You might like to create a simple slide show to show corresponding pictures of each event discussed.

A Teacher Role-Play!

I begin this first story by sharing that I am about to do something 'a bit mean.' I then select a student (who I think can handle this) and simply approach him where he is sitting and ask him to stand up. I then take his seat and leave him standing in front of the group, confused and unsure as to what he is supposed to be doing. I continue talking to the group, getting on with the lesson, ignoring the standing student…for just a quick minute. I then stop speaking and ask the student who has been left standing, 'How are you feeling right now?'

A typical response is 'embarrassed', 'a bit uncomfortable,' or sometimes a shrug, 'I don't know!'

I allow the student to sit down, then invite the whole group into a discussion. 'Does anyone know why I did that? Does anyone know at what point in time someone who was asked to stand up but who refused to do so, made history?' Most often a few students know the answer: Rosa Parks a forerunner to the Civil Rights Movement in the USA.

Now read on:

- In 1956, in Alabama, USA, a woman refused to give up her seat on a public bus. For her actions, she was arrested, fingerprinted and spent the night in jail before being bailed out the next evening by friends. For Rosa Parks, and others like her, living in a time of law-enforced segregation in the United States of America, this was her 'Almost impossible thought'—to stand up to the system that said, a black person must give up his/her seat on the bus if there was no other seat available for a white person. And now Rosa Parks had set her 'thought' in motion by the most simple of actions, by quite literally not standing up.
- Nelson Mandela was sentenced to life imprisonment on Robben Island—labelled a 'terrorist' and a 'saboteur' by the apartheid government of South Africa. After twenty-seven years of imprisonment, it was an 'Almost impossible thought' that he would ever be released, let alone be voted in as the president of the country in the first democratic elections held in South Africa in 1989.

- The Berlin Wall stood as both a symbolic and physical divide between the Communist East and capitalist West Berlin. Built in 1961 by the communists, the 'Antifascist protective wall' or 'Wall of shame', depending on which side of the wall you stood, the Berlin Wall symbolized the 'Iron Curtain' drawn between Western Europe and the Eastern Bloc nations. For millions of people, it was indeed an 'Almost impossible thought' that this wall would ever come tumbling down. And yet in 1990 the demolition began.

3. What other 'Almost impossible thoughts' in history can you think of?

Allow time for the group to share. Others you may like to include:

- In the late 1800s in the USA, it was an 'Almost impossible thought' that the country could have an African-American President. Barack Obama was elected in 2008.
- In the 1950s it was an 'Almost impossible thought' that a person would ever walk on the moon. And yet this happened by 1969.
- People openly mocked the Wright brothers and others who believed that 'flying machines' could be built. Enough said on that one!
- In Australia in 1901, USA 1919, India 1949, women could not vote, oh…and solar power was unheard of.

If all these 'Almost impossible thoughts' have become a reality, then what else can become a shining reality too? We just need to have the thoughts, believe in their possibility, and take the first steps to make them happen.

4. Where can our 'Almost impossible thoughts' take us?

Let us return for a minute to the Rosa Parks story.

Rosa Parks is one person in a chain of events that nobody could have foreseen the connections most certainly not her. For in Rosa Parks 'sitting down for her truth', her protest and the voices of others, led to what was known as the Montgomery Bus Boycott of 1955. Into this fray a young up-and-coming preacher was invited to become a spokesperson for the black civil rights cause. He was well known in his own area in southern USA, but not yet beyond. His name was Martin Luther King Jr.

As Martin Luther King's name grew into a household phrase, he was invited to speak at the Washington protest of 1963. Being one of several speakers addressing 250,000 people gathered before them, King began his speech. As he paused to finish, his friend, Mahalia Jackson, sitting behind, prompted him, 'Martin, tell them about your dream.' And King continued, his voice rising, impassioned, 'I have a dream that one day this nation will rise up and live out the true meaning of its creed: We hold these truths to be self-evident, that all men are created equal.' It is this part of the speech that is remembered and still studied by young people around the world today. Rosa Parks could not have foreseen the pathway of her 'Almost impossible thought.'

5. Using music as a pathway

There are *many* video clips highlighting 'Almost impossible thoughts' that have become incredible realities, beyond where the originator of the 'thought' believed it might travel. Select one to watch and discuss. Students may like to bring in choices of their own.

A few examples:

Nickelback: 'If Everyone Cared'. 'Official version' showing Live Aid, Nelson Mandela, Amnesty International and more.

Michael Jackson: 'Man in the Mirror' version showing Martin Luther King Jr, Gandhi, JFK, Mother Theresa, KKK, Hitler, funeral for nuclear weapons and more.

Rage Against the Machine: 'Sleep Now in the Fire' version showing Wall Street and a Game Show. This is a more contemporary band. Watch the game show closely!

The Black Eyed Peas: 'Where is the Love' version with the band posting question marks and children singing the chorus. It is definitely worth also showing the lyrics of this song and opening up for discussion.

For each song you choose, hand out and discuss the lyrics.

Discuss each example shown in the video clip. Remember to mention that each of these bands is bringing their own 'Almost impossible thoughts' into reality by writing these songs and creating these video clips.

Discuss these lyrics from Michael Jackson's song, 'Man in the Mirror'. How do these lyrics relate to Gandhi's message: Be the change you wish to see in this world?

> *I'm starting with the Man in the Mirror*
> *I'm asking him to change his ways*
> *And no message could have been any clearer*
> *If you wanna make the world*
> *A better place*

> *Take a look at yourself,*
> *And then make a change*

Discuss the healing that can come through singing. Inner and outer healing.

Teacher's note: As an ongoing activity in your classroom, invite the students to bring songs that have messages for the world, perhaps once a week. Ask them to share their thoughts and opinions about what is being said in each song.

6. It is time to dream of your 'Almost impossible thought'

This is a step-by-step process:
   What is your first step?
   There are many paths to work out your 'first step' to establishing your individual 'Almost impossible thought'. Here is one tool to help you discover yours: 'The Crossroads.'
   A friend of mine from Initiatives of Change, Australia, Rob Wood, described this simple technique to help you gain guidance in your life's direction—your life's purpose. Rob cannot recall where he first heard about the crossroads, many years ago, but since he told me about it, I have used it many times to help young people focus on their goals. It is simple and effective.

The Crossroads

Draw a horizontal line on your paper.
   Ask yourself: **What are my skills? My passions? My expertise?**
   Write them along your horizontal line, your x-axis.

Draw a vertical y-axis perpendicular to your x-axis.

Ask yourself this question, **'What does the world need me to do right now?'**

Write this on your y-axis.

Where these two lines intersect is the best place to begin your journey to step up and make a difference in this world. i.e. Where I am at right now; what can I give the world?

Examples:

My skill: I am a very good public speaker.

My passion: Animals.

Where does the world need me right now: Perhaps to present a series of talks in school forums about puppy farms, live meat exports, etc.

My skill: I am an exceptionally good soccer player.

My passion: Helping homeless people.

Where does the world need me right now: I am going to hold a soccer match fundraiser and donate the money to a charity that works for the homeless. When I am older I intend to create soccer teams in lower socio-economic areas and volunteer to teach soccer skills.

My skill: I am very good at technical drawing and spatial awareness.

My passion: To become an architect.

Where does the world need me right now: I am going to research the latest techniques for homes to be energy friendly/environmentally sustainable, then design one!

My skill: I am an excellent debater.

My passion: Social justice.

Where does the world need me right now: I am studying to be a lawyer. I am going to hold to my values of social equality. I am going to study Collaborative Law and further this path of conflict resolution in the legal system.

My skill: I am a very good writer.

My passion: Social justice.

Where does the world need me right now: I am going to join Amnesty International and put my writing skills to good use in aiding political prisoners.

Now take some 'time out', some intentional silence. (Hopefully you have begun this as a practice from Chapter Five The Conundrum of Inner Listening.) Spend 10–15 minutes in silence, allowing yourself to open up and listen to your inner voice. Ask yourself, what is it that I would like to achieve, or be part of, moving into my own future?

When those thoughts come, explore the idea of it. Firstly, say it to yourself, try it out in your own head. Secondly, say it to one other person (partner at work). Thirdly, this is your chance to say it to a large group, to have the courage to share your thoughts with others. See point 7.

7. Your idea is coming to life

Invite students, one at a time, to come up the front of the group to share their idea. Ask the student to stand slightly to the left of centre, to present their idea. Other people may ask them questions, to open up their concept. I have often seen this part of the session become a kind of debate, with students in the audience speaking in support of the idea or suggesting possible changes. This is always done respectfully.

Now, physically move this student, from a point of thought to a place of action, simply by moving them slightly to the right hand side of the audience. Ask them: What is your courageous first step towards your 'Almost impossible thought'?

When everyone who wants to present has done so, say here's 'the equation' to achieving your 'Almost impossible thought'. It's actually a simple equation, a step by step process. Let's look at how 'they' did it—Mandela, Gandhi, Jesus, Prophet Mohammed (SAWS), Mother Theresa…the people in the Nickelback clip—all of them.

First, they had an idea.

Next, they dared to share it—to say it out loud, even just to one trusted person.

Thirdly, they gathered a team around them, inspiring many people to work with them.

Then they planned their next courageous steps and took action.

And all of them, every single one of them, persevered. They never gave up, even in the face of great hardship. For some, their 'Almost impossible thought' seemed to others so impossible that sometimes they were mocked for their dreams. So hold on to this Gandhi quote: 'First they ignore you, then they laugh at you, then they fight you, then you win.'

8. Here are some 'Almost impossible thoughts'

I have heard these from participants in the *Global*

Participation—it starts with us! Student conferences and teacher workshops, run by The Gandhi Experiment:

'I am going to take more time for myself—learn to meditate; practise more often. I believe this will help me with my stress levels. And if it helps me, it will help my family.'

'There are still child marriages arranged in my family. I have been lucky that this was not me. I am going to step in to stop this from continuing in my family.'

'My community is being torn apart by serious arguing over who is the rightful leader. I'm not quite sure how just yet, but I am going to take some quiet time to think how I can contribute to a peaceful solution.'

I remember speaking with one young girl in Mumbai who was feeling quite overwhelmed by an issue tearing apart her community. We discussed the situation at length, and it was difficult to see how, at such a young age, she could become personally involved. By talking together, we came to this as a point of action: 'If there is nothing you can do about that situation, then find positive ways you can commit to building community in other ways. This will help alleviate your stress, help build better bonds of trust in the community so that hopefully such occurrences won't continue to happen in the future. And remember, we don't know where your "Almost impossible thought" may take you. It might take you to a solution to your original problem that you had never even thought of.'

9. 'Mira's email': possibilities!

A few days after holding a *Global participation—it starts with us!* conference in Melbourne, I received the following email. What was being said astounded me. I have included this email to show the power of opening up young people to the possibility of their own 'Almost impossible thoughts.' You may like to share this with your students, or simply read it for yourself. In reading it to teenagers, because it was written by a teenager, it gives them permission to speak out loud too about their ideas, about their feelings, being both honest and vulnerable. Mira has gone on to work with me, and at the age of 16 is now forming her own project by using 'The Crossroads' tool and by employing mindful action to her 'Almost impossible thought.'

Mira's email

One student's response to the *Global Participation—it starts with us!* student conference 15/04/2015, hosted by The Gandhi Experiment:

Hi Margaret,

Today I went to your *Global Participation—it starts with us*! seminar. You asked us to email you a few things about today and what we could take away from it, but even though I'm not sure how to word this entirely, I would like to tell you some things I have taken away, because your seminar completely changed my outlook on things.

You talked about anger, about revenge, and about forgiveness.

I told you I was half Palestinian, but I consider myself full as I can identify more with that side of me. I am sure you are aware of the Israeli Occupation currently happening in Palestine and this is the biggest thing in my life. The reason why I am telling you this is to explain how you changed my outlook on this situation as my original almost impossible thought was 'Palestine gets its land back, Israeli's become the ones under occupation, and we are free.'

That was my original want. It may seem mean but who can blame me after the genocide in Gaza and how I have lost family members who were shot by soldiers and have to watch as my aunt mourns for her lost son or how my cousins got into a weapon-involved fight while the soldiers stood around waiting to arrest them. It is a cruel situation and I used to think I could never forgive them for taking the life of my family members, for how they treat us at checkpoints, for how hard they make it for us to live there, in a country that was ours before them.

And yet, in the space of a day, you changed my mind.

You spoke about Malala, and how she wished education for the Taliban's children, and how she stated that she would be no better than them if she responded without peace. You spoke about Nelson Mandela and how he forgave the people who put him in jail because harbouring hate and wanting revenge is not the way to make a change.

So that got me thinking. My [Almost] impossible thought was the liberation of Palestine with punishments to the Israelis for all they have done to us. Sure, they might have pulled out couches and watched Gaza get bombed—many of them did this. BUT. If I did the same, I am no better than them, whether I have a right to revenge or not.

So now, thanks to you, my new impossible thought is not the Liberation of Palestine or the free reign of terror rights to Israel. But a new state, a new name, a new flag. No religious political party in charge, the wall separating the Muslims and Jews/Palestinians and Israelis would be knocked down. There would be no segregation of the races. Of course there would be revenge attacks on the sly, but my new [Almost] Impossible thought is peace for my people and forgiveness to the people who hurt us, because I know not all of them wanted that. I want peace and rights to my people and my family and future generations of Palestinians and Israelis.

I have yet to forgive them, but I have no interest in revenge anymore, but instead to work towards forgiveness, and most of all, peace.

But who knows, maybe one day when my [Almost] Impossible thought is a Possible one that has happened I will have the right mindset to forgive, not forget, but forgive. And that is thanks to you.

Thank you for today, it has truly, truly changed my way of thinking.

Mira.

10. Reflection

Read the following to your class:

'Mohandas Gandhi did not wish to be called the Mahatma, "Great Soul". He said, "Often the title has deeply pained me." I think what he was trying to say was that we can all do what he did, just in different ways. Now there's a wonderful "Almost impossible thought."'

To support this concept, finish with reading this passage to the class. This passage is often mistakenly attributed to Nelson Mandela, yet was actually written by Marianne Williamson in her book, *A Return to Love* (1996). It is titled 'Our Deepest Fear'. Ask the students to sit very quietly, perhaps with their eyes shut, if they are comfortable to do so. Tell them this passage is all about them.

> Our deepest fear is not that we are inadequate. Our deepest fear is that we are powerful beyond measure. It is our light, not our darkness that most frightens us. We ask ourselves, 'Who am I to be brilliant, gorgeous, talented, and fabulous?' Actually, who are you not to be? You are a child of God. Your playing small does not serve the world. There is nothing enlightened about shrinking so that other people will not feel insecure around you. We are all meant to shine, as children do. We were born to make manifest the glory of God that is within us. It is not just in some of us; it is in everyone. And as we let our own light shine, we unconsciously give others permission to do the same. As we are liberated from our own fear, our presence automatically liberates others.

Now feel the change in the room.

Teacher's Note:

You can access videoclips of 'story telling' these 'Almost impossible thoughts' and 'Walking through the "Almost impossible thoughts equation"' at www.thegandhiexperiment.com.

You may like to do further research on:

- Gandhi's policies of non-cooperation

- Nelson Mandela
- The Berlin Wall—creation and demolition
- Rosa Parks
- Martin Luther King—I have a dream
- The connection between Gandhi, Martin Luther King Jr and Nelson Mandela
- How Amnesty International began
- The formation of 'Live Aid' 1985

Conclusion

LET'S pause for a moment to consider a few things, particularly around the relevance of Gandhi in education today. If we can view education beyond the bounds of the walls of our schools; if we don't isolate the notion of education to students and teachers; if we can see that education and society—building community—are inextricably part of each other; then we will also understand the relevance of Gandhi's philosophies of actively teaching respect, non-violence, stepping up to injustice, understanding the importance of 'my role', teaching to be less competitive, non-adversarial, less materialistic, learning by doing, to see the good in humanity and the commonality in all. Let's try a little exercise.

Where does this quote come from?

> *This is the sum of duty: do not do to others what would cause pain if done to you.*
>
> HINDU TEXT—Mahabharata 5:1517

Then what about this?

> *None of you [truly] believes until he wishes for his brother what he wishes for himself.*
>
> ISLAMIC—NUMBER 13 OF IMAM
> Al-Nawawi's *Forty Hadiths.*

And this?

> *Hurt not others in ways that you yourself would find hurtful.*
>
> BUDDHIST-UDANA-VARGA 5:18

> *...and don't do what you hate...*
>
> CHRISTIAN—GOSPEL OF THOMAS 6

> *What is hateful to you, do not to your fellow man.*
> *This is the law: all the rest is commentary.*
>
> JUDAISM—TALMUD, SHABBAT 31A

> *A man should wander about treating all creatures*
> *as he himself would be treated.*
>
> JAINISM—SUTRAKRITANGA 1.11.33

> *And if thine eyes be turned towards justice, choose thou for thy*
> *neighbour that which thou choosest for thyself.*
>
> BAHAI—EPISTLE TO THE SON OF THE WOLF

Are we getting the picture? All these 'different' religions are saying the same thing. They are sending out the same message—about respect, about how we should treat others – in the way we wish to be treated.

And then there's this:

> *All things are our relatives; what we do to everything, we do to*
> *ourselves. All is really One.*
>
> NATIVE AMERICAN SPIRITUALITY–BLACK ELK

(Source: http://www.religioustolerance.org/reciproc2.htm)

If you are not religious, the concept of treating others how you like to be treated yourself surely still has very real application. We need to apply this by opening our eyes well beyond the confines of our neighbours, or even the village, town or city in which we live. Let's think globally. If I want my children to receive a good education, why would I want anyone else's children not to? If I wish to buy that new dress, or that chocolate bar or that new car, am I in some way harming someone or something else? How do I apply Gandhi's 'My life is my message', not just by being nice to my friends, but by understanding *my role* in the chopping down of the Brazilian Rainforest? (Yes, you read that correctly.)

I recall a friend, Mary Whiteside, telling a small group that 'change is possible in human beings'. That is a grand thought if you bring it deep inside yourself, because it means change is possible in 'me'. It is also the crux of Gandhism. Mary went on to tell us a story about a young man who had been part of the Taliban who no longer believed in acts of violence to validate his own purpose for living. He was travelling the world to share his story of change.

My life is my message. Politicians cannot be yelling 'We want peace!' and yet declare war, dropping bombs and allowing the sale of arms. That is what George Orwell would have termed 'double-think'. Likewise, celebrities cannot yell, 'Say no to violence', or lend themselves to anti-violence campaigns and yet continue to star in movies that stylize violence or make violence 'sexy'. And above and beyond all of this, *we* cannot sit back and pin everything on everyone else. If you wish to be part of positive change, you really need to ask yourself, what is it about *me* that needs to change? What is my sugar? (The answer may very well start with...well...sugar!)

If change begins with me, how can I expect others to change if I haven't managed to change myself? As teachers and parents, we have the capacity to open our children, and ourselves, to this way of thinking, acting, doing.

'A New Dawn'
Malathi Karpur—Zentangle artist

The Songlines

I sing a song
in existential time
A song of pathways

LANDSCAPE OF DREAMING

We tred our path; our way is known
A new world awaits
A new wealth awaits
Shared in the song of abundance,
by all

MARGARET HEPWORTH 2016

Endnotes

Further material supporting the activities in this book can be found at: www.thegandhiexperiment.com

Free lessons online

These lessons are continually growing. Feel free to write and make a suggestion about lesson content you would like to receive.

Paid lessons online

All paid lessons are kept deliberately inexpensive. This money allows The Gandhi Experiment to continue with its many important educational projects. It also helps support new authors, poets and artists such as:

Robert New, 'How to Win a War'—a short story. Robert is the author of *Incite Insight*, Tale Publishers, 2016 www.talepublishing.com

Susan Stewart, poet and artist: 'No More Crucifixion'

Collaborative Debating: A refreshing, new framework for debating. 'Debating without conflict,' where the win is the solution to the problem.

Videoclips/readings for use in the classroom or at home at www.thegandhiexperiment.com

Story-telling 'Almost impossible thoughts'
    Where can our 'Almost impossible thoughts' take us?
    Walking through the 'Almost impossible thoughts' equation
    The Crossroads
    Einstein's Theory of Why? Why? Why?—using various situations and examples to help you explore the use of the technique, including:

What is the root cause of war?
Why? Why? Why? A case study in domestic violence.

Exploring The Utopian Scale
    Guided meditations

Invitation to speak at your school or forum

Student conference: *Global participation—it starts with us!*
    Teacher workshops: How to teach global citizenship, conflict resolution, anger management and positivity for a better future.
    Parent Seminars: Thriving Teens: Building relationship between you and your teenagers
    Keynote speaker: For your conference or seminar

I am prepared to go where I am needed. And to where I can continue to learn, share and revel in the rich company of other teachers, parents and most of all, the students. Invite me to your school—yes, anywhere in this world!

YouTube clips

Education today is our society tomorrow. https://www.youtube.com/watch?v=lWqb0yEEX5Y

Resource list

An ever-growing resource list is available on my website www.

thegandhiexperiment.com

Feedback-invitation to share your thoughts

Do you have questions/thoughts/opinions? In education? In business? Send them to margaret@margarethepworth.com

Contact details

Website: www.thegandhiexperiment.com
Email: margaret@margarethepworth.com
Facebook: https://www.facebook.com/TheGandhiExperiment/
Twitter: @Marghepworth
Linkedin: Margaret Hepworth

Mindful activism

Mindful activism is the practice of taking action towards your goal to 'make a positive difference'. Whilst doing so, be mindful, or aware, of every part of the equation, who is it affecting: people, the planet? Hold to the mantra, 'if I win, you win too'. Above all, be self-aware and listen to your inner voice for guidance. It is about underpinning your actions for change with your deepest values and being courageous enough to hold on to these!

It is also the title of my sequel: *The Gandhi Experiment— Teaching our Teenagers Mindful Activism.*

Permissions and references

Permissions have been granted for use of the following:

Excerpt from Leonard Zunin MD and Natalie Zunin (1972), *Contact: The First Four Minutes*, Ballantine Books, granted by Sobel Weber Associates, Inc. New York.

Sharing the illuminating story of the Babemba Tribe. Sheryl 'Shera' Sever, Igniting the Spark, www.sherylsever.com. http://

sherylsever.com/2007/11/know-your-song-and-sing-it/Impactful writing in relation to the Babemba Tribe

Jessica Hilltout, photographer. From her project, AMEN-Grassroots Football. The photo used in this book for *The Best Forgiveness Role-Play Ever* is of Abukari from Kpenjipei in Northern Ghana. 'The image is a spontaneous moment captured after an intense football match. In these areas football is not just a game it is one of life's essentials.' At the time of writing, Abdul-Ganiyu Abubakari is setting out to locate Abukari to let him know the impact this photo has already had on thousands of teachers and students alike. I am sure it will continue to do so.

Marianne Williamson: 'Our Deepest Fear' passage from her book *A Return to Love,* HarperCollins Publishers, 1996. This quote has become famously used worldwide, and invariably misquoted as having been said by Nelson Mandela. Rather than take umbrage with this, Marianne simply says she is grateful the quote has meant so much to so many.

Susan Stewart, poet and artist. Poem: '*A New World*' from *Moonlight Meanderings.* And other beautiful quotes accessed from her inner voice. moad57@hotmail.com

Dilip Patel, certified Zentangle teacher and Life Purpose workshops' facilitator. For the inspiring drawing—'Be the change.' www.facebook.com/zentanglewithdilippatel, dilip.patel@gmail.com

Malathi Karpur, Zentangle inspired art, for her intriguing artwork, *A New Dawn*, which appeared to me just as I was researching the Songlines. http://xploreandxpress.blogspot.in/2013/07/zentangle-challenge-125-z-inspiration-1.html, xploreandxpress@gmail.com

James Tyler, Darcy Tyler, Artist/Photographer. 'BP Look what you've done to me,' 2012, inviting us all to take action.

Bernadette Hugh-Clink, healer medium, for her insightful quotes from her inner voice.

April Cameron. Photograph—'Time out.' Lateral thinking in parenting.

Mira's Email—in *Almost Impossible Thoughts*. Permission has been granted by Mira, who at this point in her young life, chooses to remain anonymous. Poignant and moving.

Sincere thanks to all of you.

References

Education Today, Society Tomorrow (ETST)—Initiatives of Change, India. This group of dedicated educators hold two annual workshops for teachers at Panchgani, India. They believe social transformation begins with personal transformation. I have been presenting workshops there for the last two years and hope to continue to do so. http://in.iofc.org/etst

Cheryl Wood, Rob Wood, Mary Whiteside—Initiatives of Change, Australia. Building trust across the world's divides. http://au.iofc.org

James Tyler—Life education through a holistic approach.

Genevieve Sovereign—Conscious enterprise communications specialist. http://gsovereign.com.au/

Eckart Tolle, A New Earth, Penguin Group, 2005.

Dr Ghanshyam Sharma is a prestigious yoga teacher in Mumbai, India. www.yogaspaceme.comdrgbsharma@hotmail.com

Chintan Girish Modi, friend, writer who believes in the possibility of friendships across cultural differences and political borders.

Fischer, L. (1983), *The Essential Gandhi*, Vintage Books, Random House: New York.

Bakshi, R. *The Guardian*, Jan 2013. http://www.theguardian.com/sustainable-business/blog/relevance-gandhi-capitalism-debate-rajni-bakshi

Positive Psychology—www.positivepsychologyinstitute.com.au
Religious Tolerance—http://www.religioustolerance.org
Nai Talim—www.gandhifoundation.net
Freddie Mercury, David Bowie, *Under Pressure*; 1981, EMI Elektra
Michael Jackson, *Man in the Mirror,* 1988. Written by Siedah Garret and Glen Ballard. Produced by Quincy Jones and Michael Jackson.
Conflict Resolution Network—http://www.crnhq.org. An interesting example of a shift in the dominant paradigm and discovering the collective consciousness. A friend told me that an activity very similar to a new educational tool I created, *Collaborative Debating*, could be found on this site. When I checked, I discovered the CRN Conflict Resolving Game to be remarkably alike in structure and intent. I spoke with one of the women involved in setting up this wonderful website which offers many free resources for people looking for conflict resolution activities. We shared our thoughts and decided that many, many times, have more than one person come up with the same idea. We agreed that getting these ideas out to the world was the most important thing. Please peruse the CRN website and its wonderful offerings.
Margaret Hepworth (2012), *Clarity in Time*, Balboa Press. Excerpts have been taken and used to shape activities.
Edward de Bono is a critical thinker and author of Six Thinking Hats. He coined the term 'Parallel Thinking' and postulates this as a way forward in seeking solutions through a lateral approach.

Acknowledgements

No one stands alone in their achievements; we are all products of teamwork.

Such a simple and obvious statement—yet it resonates deeply with the core of this book. As I sought permission from people across continents, to use their photos, quotes, poems, drawings and passages in my book, the responses came rolling in—'Yes', 'Certainly', 'Absolutely'. I could clearly see the momentum of affirmative messages growing in leaps and bounds across this planet, a movement away from 'It's mine', 'I own this, you can't have it'. People are increasingly collaborating with those they have never met, or even heard of; no introductions from someone else, just a request and a mutual understanding that cooperation makes this world a better place. As photographer Jessica Hilltout put it to me, 'We know in our hearts we are doing the right thing.'

Thank you to every one of you.

There are many more to thank for *The Gandhi Experiment: Teaching our teenagers how to become global citizens* coming to fruition. This most certainly includes the students who have approached me after the workshops to share their valued feedback. To Mira, Jameela, Anya, and all of you who have emailed telling me what you now feel inspired to do. I don't think you could possibly understand how that motivates me to go on.

My team of friends, helping with the book, spans Australia, India, Pakistan, Germany and Fiji. They are my proof readers and encouragers. They are testament to the way we can utilize the internet as a positive tool to create a global village. Some of them tested the activities; others read and made detailed critiques of the technicalities of writing and of the concepts; some read, then encouraged with glorious enthusiasm. To Chintan Girish Modi, Deepika Shell, Vipul Shaha, Joanne Chappell, Genevieve Sovereign, JensAugspurger, Amit Deshwal, Anam Zakaria, Kalara Une, Urmila Samson, Cailean Douglas, Sasha Buntman and my young friend, Mira, thank you! Chintan you have such dedication and commitment; you are a visionary, a character, a confidant and dear friend. Your expression, 'Don't be jealous, be joyous', has never failed to hit home for me.

To my meditation group led by Bernadette Hugh-Clink; to all in the group for the energy raised, and for allowing my conscious and unconscious to meet with surprising clarity. People who know and understand synchronicity will not be surprised to hear the following story. As I travelled across India, holding student and teacher workshops, people would ask me, 'What is your next step?' I told them, 'I want to publish these activities so they can be accessed by teachers and parents worldwide.' I came home to Australia to discover that an email had been sitting in my unopened inbox for ten days. It was from Dharini Bhaskar of Rupa Publications. 'I have read about your work and we are wondering, would you like to write a book about "The Gandhi Experiment"?' I nearly fell off my chair. Dharini, Amrita and the team at Rupa have encouraged, explained, answered every little question and most of all, formed a friendship across the airwaves. Sincere thanks for this 'no coincidences' finding of me!

Sandra Maxfield, Trish Hepworth, Mike Hepworth, Natasha Girvan and Srijoy Das—each know the important role they played. The ETST team in India continues to allow me to explore ideas for peace education at their annual teachers' workshops in Panchgani, India. If you ever get the chance, come join us!

To many friends and family, especially Jo, Ildi, Naz and Robbie, who always tell me that they are proud of me.

To the gorgeous Mumtazullah, for dinners that walked in the door to sustain me and the constant, loving encouragement. My children, James and Darcy, who walk alongside me on this journey with a depth of support I find difficult to describe.

I thank you all.

Finally, throughout this book, you will read quotes and messages from famous and ordinary people alike. As this is the Acknowledgements section, I would like *you* to acknowledge two things:

1. All these 'famous' people were 'ordinary' people once; indeed, they would all still claim such average—no different to you and me—status.
2. When you read the quotes or poems or view the artwork of the so-called 'ordinary' people, I hope you will acknowledge this as evidence that *all of us have such inner wisdom*. There is depth to each and every one of us. To explore this is the greatest adventure of our lives.